GET READY
FOR SCHOOL:
KINDERGARTEN

HEATHER STELLA

593 ACTIVITIES & **3,835** ILLUSTRATIONS

BLACK DOG
& LEVENTHAL
PUBLISHERS
NEW YORK

Black Dog & Leventhal Publishers
Hachette Book Group
1290 Avenue of the Americas
New York, NY 10104
www.hachettebookgroup.com
www.blackdogandleventhal.com

First edition: May 2016
First revised and updated edition: April 2020

Black Dog & Leventhal Publishers is an imprint of Perseus Books, LLC,
a subsidiary of Hachette Book Group, Inc. The Black Dog & Leventhal
Publishers name and logo are trademarks of Hachette Book Group, Inc.

The Hachette Speakers Bureau provides a wide range
of authors for speaking events. To find out more, go to
www.HachetteSpeakersBureau.com or call (866) 376-6591.

LCCN: 2019944328

ISBN: 978-0-7624-6990-1

Printed in China

APS

10 9 8 7 6 5 4 3 2 1

CONTENTS

A NOTE TO PARENTS

GET READY FOR SCHOOL: KINDERGARTEN is an indispensable educational companion for your pre-kindergarten child. It is chock-full of fun, interesting, curriculum-based activities—such as those focusing on the alphabet, numbers, colors, shapes, math readiness, nature, and more—that will introduce your child to new concepts while reinforcing what he or she already knows. In addition, there are plenty of fun word games, mazes, and coloring activities that are designed to entertain and amuse your child while boosting his or her basic skills.

We recommend setting aside some time each day to read with your child. The more your child reads, the faster he or she will acquire other skills. We also suggest that you have your child complete a portion of the book each day. You and your child can sit down and discuss what the goals for each day will be, and perhaps even choose a reward to be given upon completion of the whole book—such as a trip to the park, a special playdate, or something else that seems appropriate to you. While you want to help your child set educational goals, be sure to offer lots of encouragement along the way. These activities are not meant as a test. By making them fun and rewarding, you will help your child look forward to completing them, and he or she will be especially eager to tackle the educational challenges ahead!

Hey, kids!
Remember to have
a pencil, some crayons,
stickers, glue, and
popsicle sticks handy when
playing with your
Get Ready book!

ALPHABET

Tall, Small, and Fall Letters

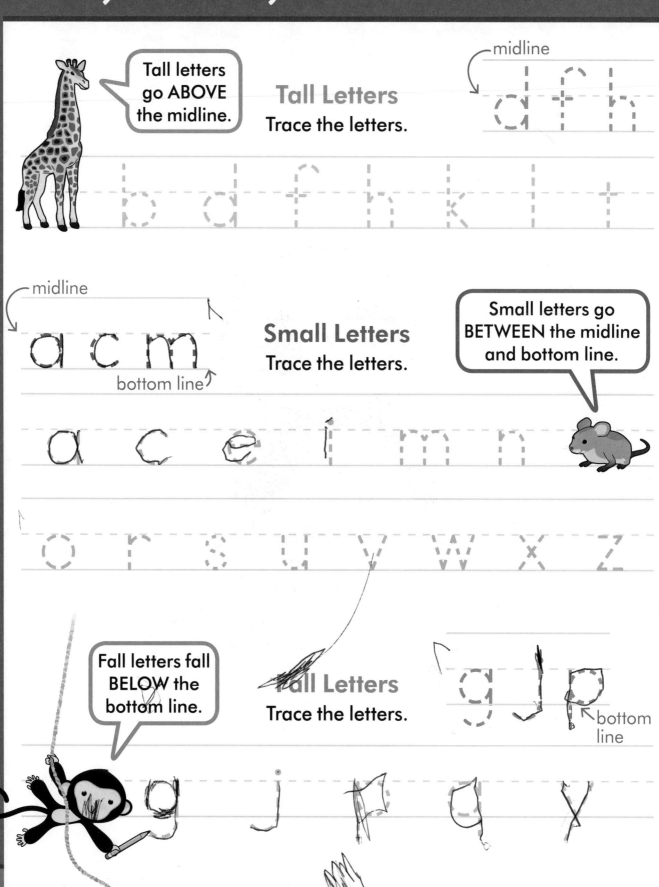

Tall letters go ABOVE the midline.

Tall Letters
Trace the letters.

midline

d f h

b d f h k l t

midline

a c m

bottom line

Small Letters
Trace the letters.

Small letters go BETWEEN the midline and bottom line.

a c e i m n

o r s u y w x z

Fall letters fall BELOW the bottom line.

Fall Letters
Trace the letters.

g j p

bottom line

g j p q y

Tall, Small, and Fall Letters

Write the letters from the letter box under
the correct category (fall, tall, or small letters).

b p r y k f h
m z g d j e s q

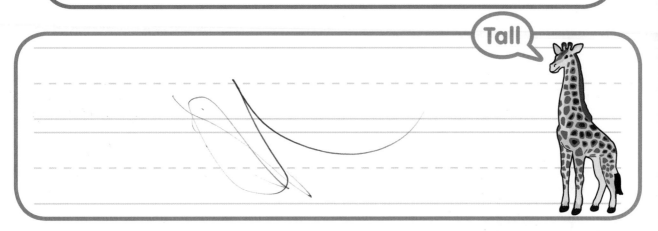

Tall

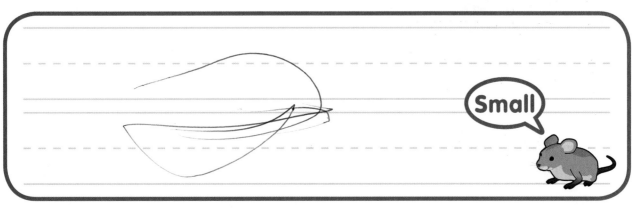

Small

Fall

11

Uppercase Letter A

A is for _____ PPLE. Trace the uppercase letter **A**.
Then try writing it on your own.

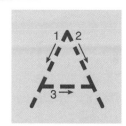  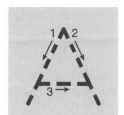  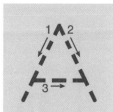

start

Help the **A**lligator get to the water by following
the path of uppercase letter **A**.

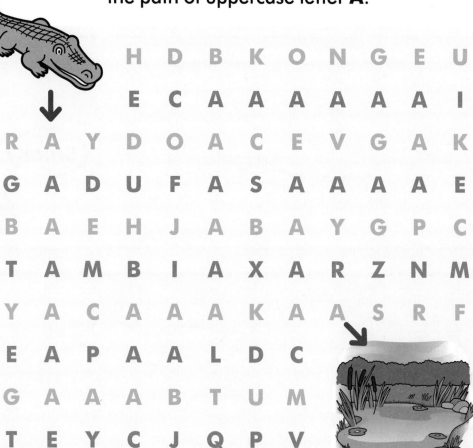

H	D	B	K	O	N	G	E	U
	E	C	A	A	A	A	A	I
R	A	Y	D	O	A	C	E	V	G	A	K
G	A	D	U	F	A	S	A	A	A	A	E
B	A	E	H	J	A	B	A	Y	G	P	C
T	A	M	B	I	A	X	A	R	Z	N	M
Y	A	C	A	A	A	K	A	A	S	R	F
E	A	P	A	A	L	D	C
G	A	A	A	B	T	U	M
T	E	Y	C	J	Q	P	V

Lowercase Letter a

Trace the lowercase letter **a**.
Then try writing it on your own.

start

Write the beginning letter **a** to complete the words.

 _nt

 _pple

 _corn

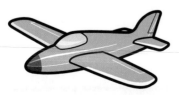 _irplane

Beginning Sounds

ANT 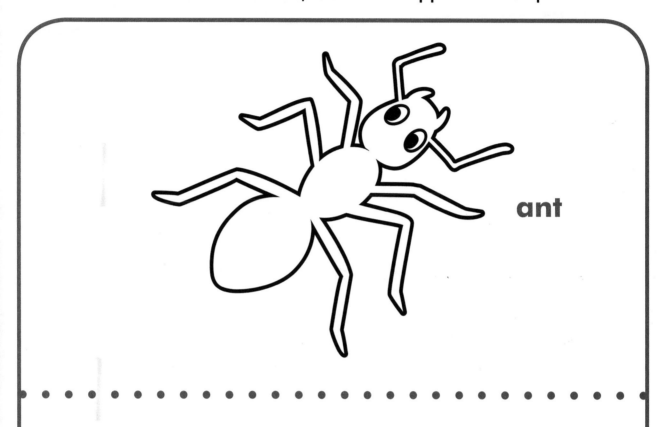 begins with the letter **A**.
Color the **a**nt. Then draw your own picture of something
that starts with the letter **A**, such as an **a**pple or an **a**irplane.

ant

Uppercase Letter B

B is for _____**EAR**. Trace the uppercase letter **B**.
Then try writing it on your own.

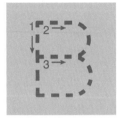 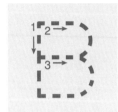 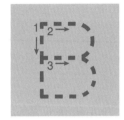 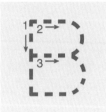 

start

B is for **BUTTERFLY**. Circle the letter **B**'s within the outlines.
Color the picture to make your own **b**utterfly.

15

Lowercase Letter b

Trace the lowercase letter **b**.
Then try writing it on your own.

start

 **B** is for **b**ird. Draw a line from the uppercase letter **B**'s to the lowercase letter **b**'s.

B   F   P   B   B

d   b   b   r   b

Beginning Sounds

Circle the picture that has the same beginning sound as the first one.

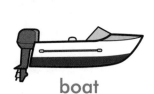

boat

sun

carrot

deer

car

bed

Uppercase Letter C

C is for ____AR.  Trace the uppercase letter **C**.
Then try writing it on your own.

start

C is for **COW**. Color the letter **C**.
Color the **c**ow.

Lowercase Letter c

Trace the lowercase letter **c**.
Then try writing it on your own.

start

C is for **CIRCLE**. Find your way to the center of this **c**ircle maze.

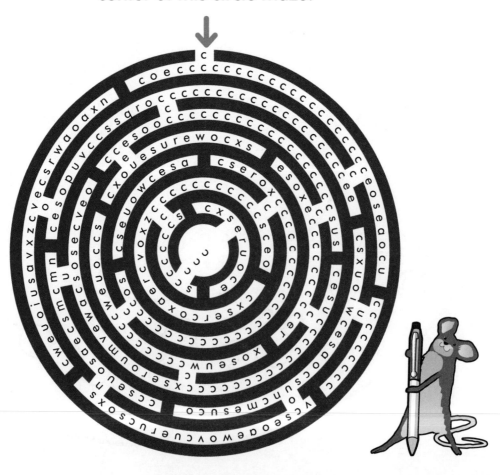

Beginning Sounds

Say the word **cat**. **Cat** starts with the **C** sound.
Color any pictures below that begin with the **C** sound.

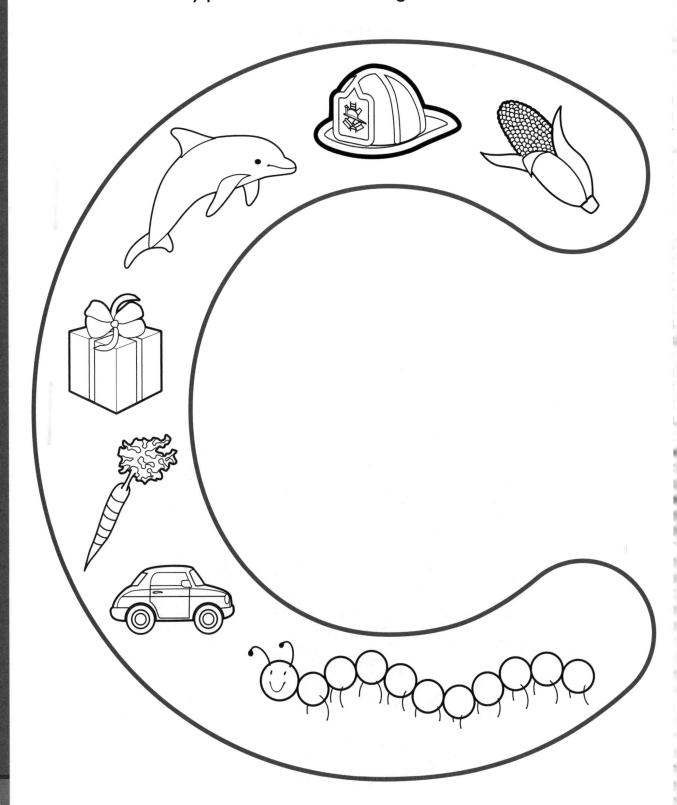

Uppercase Letter D

D is for _____UCK.  Trace the uppercase letter **D**.
Then try writing it on your own.

start

Fill in the missing **D** to complete the words.

 D is for _____OG

 **D** is for _____OLL

 **D** is for _____INOSAUR

 **D** is for _____OUGHNUT

Lowercase Letter d

Trace the lowercase letter **d**.
Then try writing it on your own.

start

Draw a line from each of the uppercase **D**'s on the **d**ucks to
one of the lowercase **d**'s on the **d**ucklings below.

Beginning Sounds

Say the word **dog**. **Dog** starts with the **D** sound. Say the name of each picture. Circle all of the pictures that begin with the **D** sound.

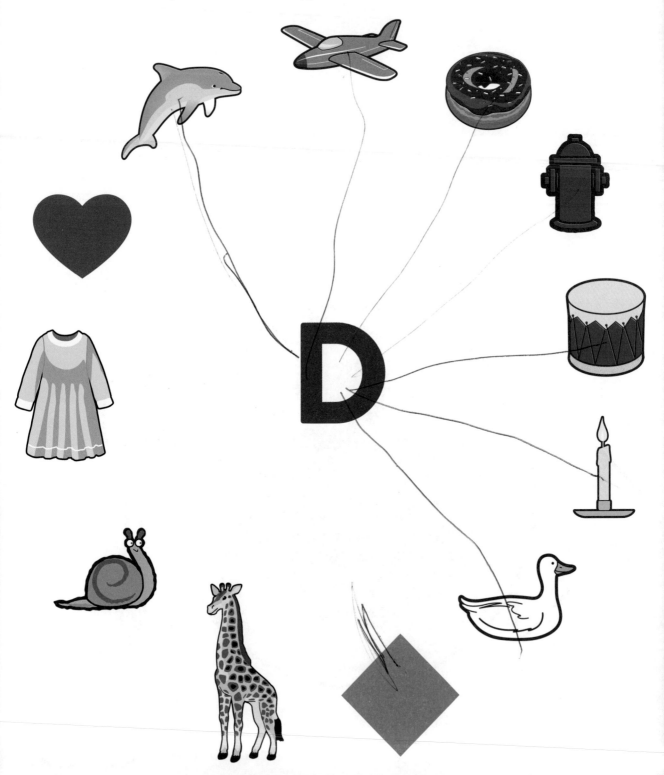

Uppercase Letter E

E is for **_____GGS**.  Trace the uppercase letter **E**.
Then try writing it on your own.

start

Color all of the uppercase **E**'s.

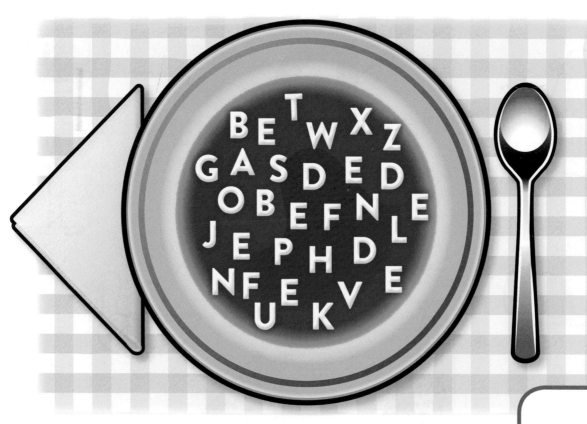

How many **E**'s
did you find?

Lowercase Letter e

Trace the lowercase letter **e**.
Then try writing it on your own.

start

Circle the words that begin
with the lowercase letter **e**.

ear	bat	bed	with
car	won	bet	eat
wig	egg	ten	see

25

Beginning Sounds

Say the name of each picture. Circle the picture that begins with the sound of the letter in each row.

Aa

Bb

Cc

Dd

Ee

F is for _____ LY. 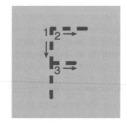 Trace the uppercase letter **F**.
Then try writing it on your own.

   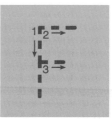

start

Find and circle all of the uppercase **F**'s in the large **F**.

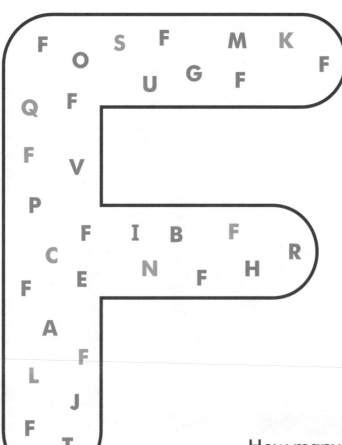

How many **F**'s
did you find?

27

Lowercase Letter f

Trace the lowercase letter **f**.
Then try writing it on your own.

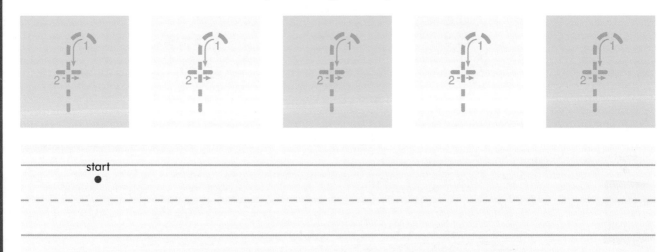

start

Help the **f**irefighter get to the **f**ire truck through the maze.

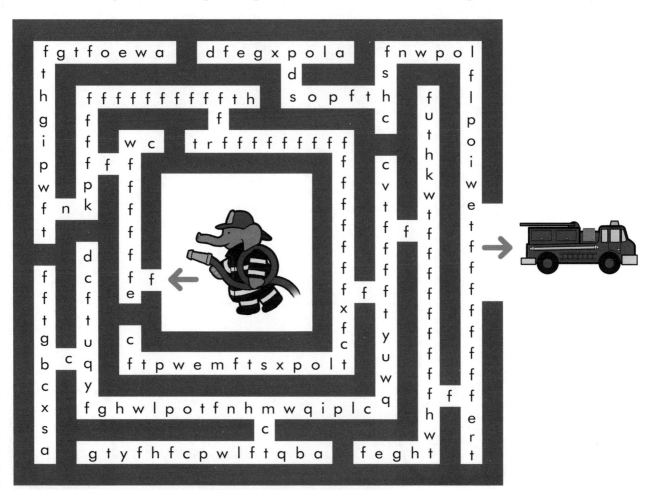

Beginning Sounds

Frog  begins with the letter **F**.
Color the **f**rog. Then draw your own picture of something
that starts with the letter **F**, such as a **f**ox or a **f**oot.

frog

Uppercase Letter G

G is for _____**IFT**. 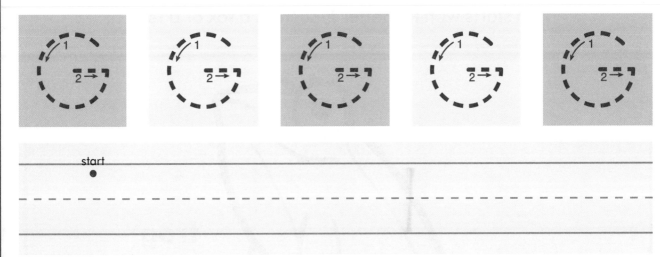 Trace the uppercase letter **G**.
Then try writing it on your own.

start

G is for **GOAT**.
Color the letter **G**. Color the **g**oat.

Lowercase Letter g

Trace the lowercase letter **g**.
Then try writing it on your own.

start

Earth is made up of land and water.
Color anything with the uppercase **G** green
and anything with the lowercase **g** blue.

31

Beginning Sounds

Say the word **grapes**. **G**rapes starts with the **G** sound.
Color any pictures that begin with the **G** sound.

Uppercase Letter H

H is for **HAT**. 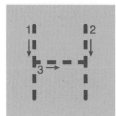 Trace the uppercase letter **H**.
Then try writing it on your own.

start

H is for **HEART**. Find your way through the **heart** maze.

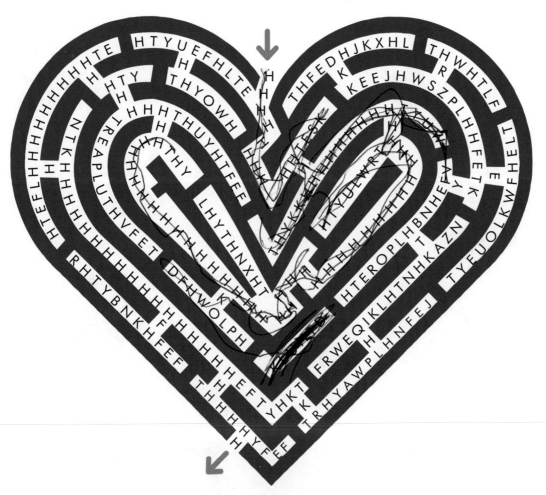

Lowercase Letter h

Trace the lowercase letter **h**.
Then try writing it on your own.

start

Draw a line from each uppercase **H** to a lowercase **h**.

Beginning Sounds

Say the word **h**oney.  **H**oney starts with the **H** sound.
Say the name of each picture. Circle all of the pictures
that begin with the **H** sound.

H

Uppercase Letter I

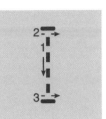

I is for _____**CE CREAM**. Trace the uppercase letter **I**.
Then try writing it on your own.

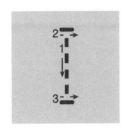   

start

Ice cream begins with the letter **I**. Connect the dots
from **A** to **I** to make your own ice-cream cone.
Color it to match your favorite flavor.

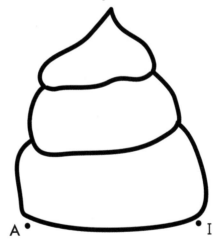

A •   • I

B • •   • • H
  C   G

D •   •   • F
           E

Lowercase Letter i

Trace the lowercase letter **i**.
Then try writing it on your own.

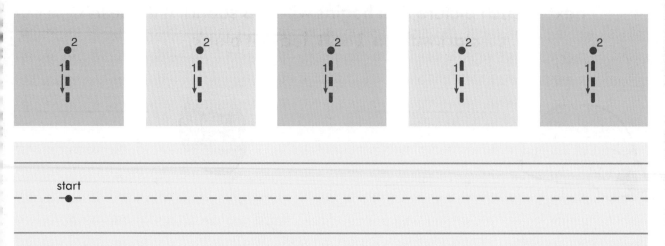

start

Color all of the ice-cream cones
that have a lowercase **i** in them.

Beginning Sounds

Say the name of each picture. Write the uppercase letter **I** next to each picture that starts with an **I** and an uppercase letter **B** next to each picture that begins with a **B** sound. If it doesn't start with an **I** or **B**, leave it blank.

Uppercase Letter J

J is for _____ELLY. Trace the uppercase letter **J**.
Then try writing it on your own.

    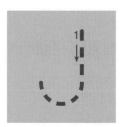

start

Fill in the missing **J** to complete the words.

 UICE

 ____UMP ROPE

 ELLY BEANS

 ACKET

Lowercase Letter j

Trace the lowercase letter **j**.
Then try writing it on your own.

  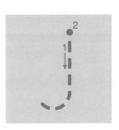  

start

Circle all of the lowercase **j**'s in the sign below.

jar	jog	lot
jaw	jet	joy
jet	fun	job

Beginning Sounds

Say the word **jaguar**.  **Jaguar** starts with the **J** sound.
Color any pictures that begin with the **J** sound.

Uppercase Letter K

K is for _____ITE. Trace the uppercase letter **K**.
Then try writing it on your own.

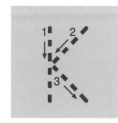  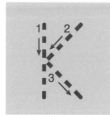 

start

Color all of the uppercase **K**'s.

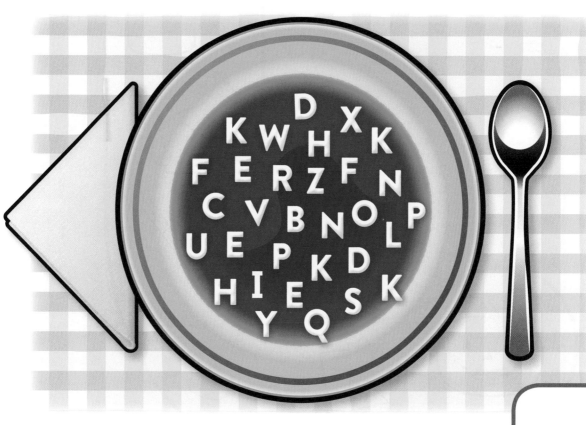

How many **K**'s
did you find?

Lowercase Letter k

Trace the lowercase letter **k**.
Then try writing it on your own.

start

Circle all of the lowercase **k**'s.
Connect the circles to complete the picture.

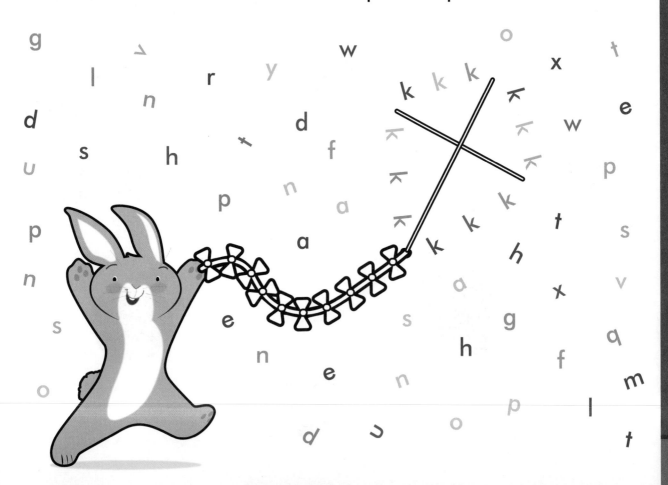

Beginning Sounds

Say the word **k**itten. **K**itten starts with the **K** sound. Say the name of each picture. Circle all of the pictures that begin with the **K** sound.

Uppercase Letter L

L is for _____ EAF. Trace the uppercase letter **L**.
Then try writing it on your own.

 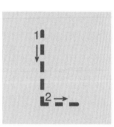  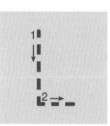 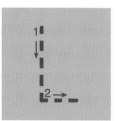

start

L is for **LION**. Color the **L**. Color the lion.

45

Lowercase Letter l

Trace the lowercase letter **l**.
Then try writing it on your own.

start

It's fall! Look how beautiful the leaves are!
Color any leaf with an uppercase **L** orange
and any leaf with a lowercase **l** red.

Beginning Sounds

Say the name of each picture. Draw a line to the letter that shows the beginning sound.

C

A

B

D

L

K

H

47

Uppercase Letter M

M is for _____ ILK. 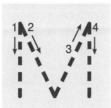 Trace the uppercase letter M.
Then try writing it on your own.

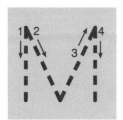 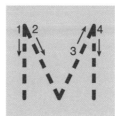 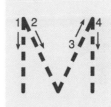 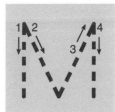

start

Color all of the uppercase M's.

How many M's
did you find?

Lowercase Letter m

Trace the lowercase letter **m**.
Then try writing it on your own.

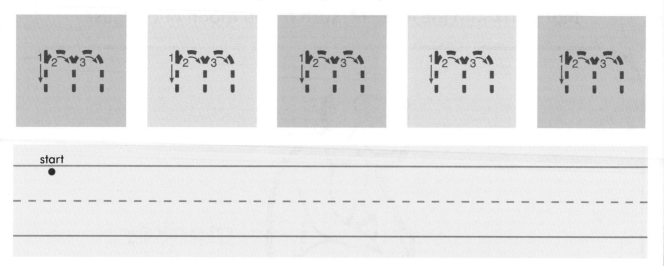

start

Draw a line from each uppercase **M** to a lowercase **m** below.

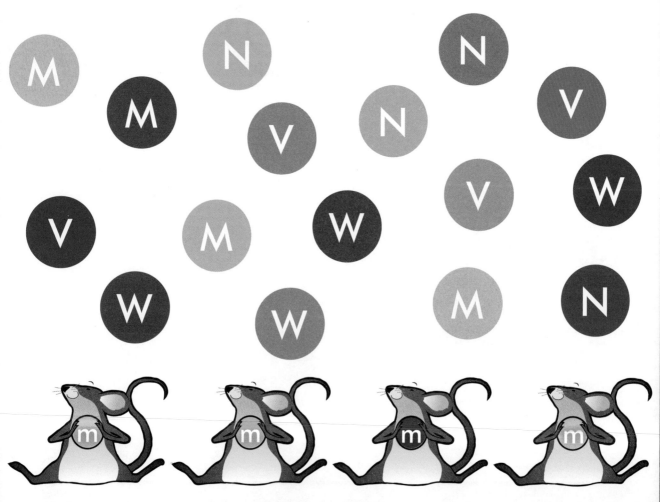

Beginning Sounds

Monkey  begins with the letter **M**.
Color the **m**onkey. Then draw your own picture of something
that starts with the letter **M**, such as the **m**oon or a **m**ouse.

monkey

N is for _____**EST**. 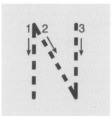 Trace the uppercase letter **N**.
Then try writing it on your own.

  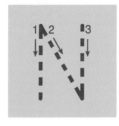 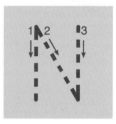

start

Find and circle all of the uppercase **N**'s in the large **N**.

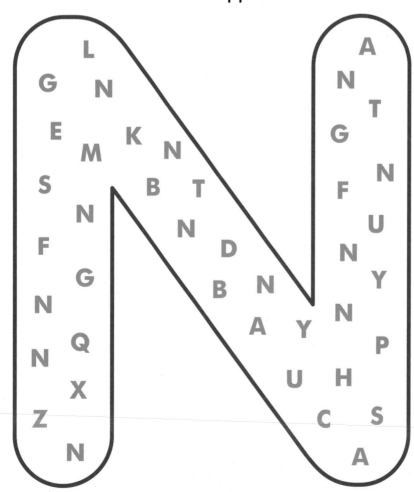

How many **N**'s
did you find?

Lowercase Letter n

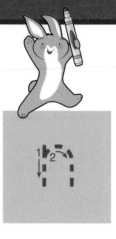

Trace the lowercase letter **n**.
Then try writing it on your own.

start

Write the beginning letter lowercase **n** to complete the words.

_____ ecklace

_____ ewspapers

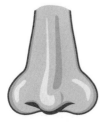

_____ ose

Beginning Sounds

Say the word **n**est. **N**est starts with the **N** sound.
Say the name of each picture. Circle all of the pictures
that begin with the same **N** sound.

53

Uppercase Letter O

O is for _____**CTOPUS**. 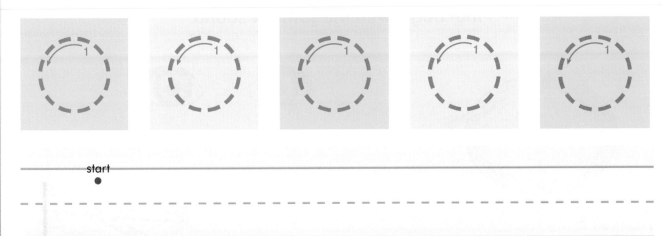 Trace the uppercase letter **O**.
Then try writing it on your own.

start

Help **O**llie the **O**wl find all of the uppercase **O**'s.
Circle each **O** that you find.

How many **O**'s
did you find?

Lowercase Letter o

Trace the lowercase letter **o**.
Then try writing it on your own.

start

Find three words in a row that begin with
the lowercase letter **o**. You can go across, down,
or diagonally. Circle all of the letter **o**'s.

one	you	mop
out	pop	ran
own	hen	not

Beginning Sounds

Say the word **O**wl. **O**wl starts with the **O** sound.
Color any pictures that begin with the **O** sound.

P is for _____EAR.  Trace the uppercase letter **P**.
Then try writing it on your own.

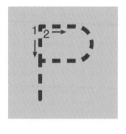 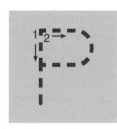  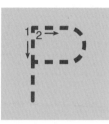

start

P is for **PIG**. Color the letter **P**. Color the **pig**.

Lowercase Letter p

Trace the lowercase letter **p**.
Then try writing it on your own.

start

Circle all of the lowercase letter **p**'s in the sign below.
Underline any words that begin with the letter **p**.

pat	pop	top	car
zap	cow	pea	why
pan	lap	pin	one

Ending Sounds

Look at each picture and say the word out loud.
What ending sound do you hear? Write the letter
in the box below each picture.

n f t l m r y x

Uppercase Letter Q

Q is for _____**UEEN**.  Trace the uppercase letter **Q**.
Then try writing it on your own.

start

Help the **QUEEN** get to her castle by following
the path of uppercase letter **Q**.

Lowercase Letter q

Trace the lowercase letter **q**.
Then try writing it on your own.

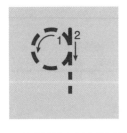    

start

Help color the beautiful quilt.
Color all the uppercase **Q**'s **red** and all the lowercase **q**'s **blue**.

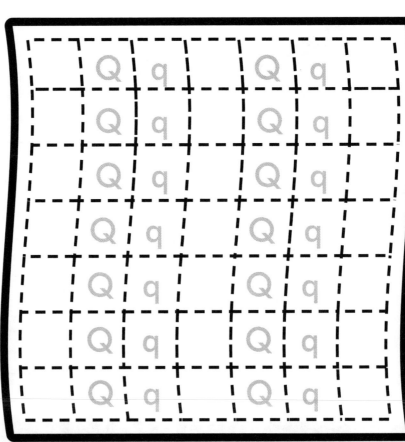

Ending Sounds

Write the missing letter for the ending sound.

n r t p d g

robo ___

scoote ___

skateboar ___

swin ___

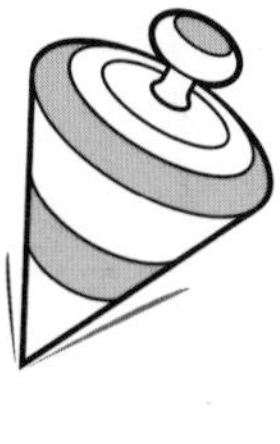

to ___

wago ___

Uppercase Letter R

ALPHABET

R is for _____**OCKET**.  Trace the uppercase letter **R**.
Then try writing it on your own.

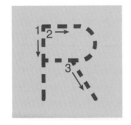   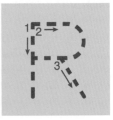

start

R is for **ROCKET**. Circle all of the uppercase **R**'s below.

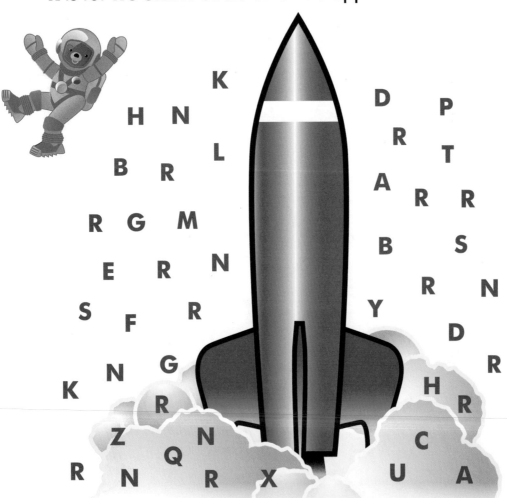

63

Lowercase Letter r

Trace the lowercase letter **r**.
Then try writing it on your own.

start

Color all of the raindrops with the lowercase **r** blue.

Beginning Sounds

Robot begins with the letter **R**. Color the robot. Then draw your own picture of something that starts with the letter **R**, such as a **r**ooster or a **r**abbit.

robot

Uppercase Letter S

Trace the uppercase letter **S**.
Then try writing it on your own.

start

Snake begins with the letter **S**.
Find and color all of the **s**nakes in the picture below.

How many **s**nakes did you find?

Lowercase Letter s

Trace the lowercase letter **s**.
Then try writing it on your own.

start

Color any spider with the lowercase **s black**.

Beginning Sounds

Say the word **s**un. **S**un starts with the **S** sound.
Color any pictures that begin with the **S** sound in the large **S**.

Uppercase Letter T

T is for _____OP. 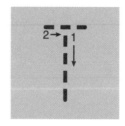 Trace the uppercase letter **T**.
Then try writing it on your own.

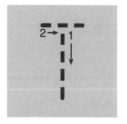   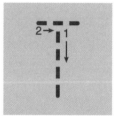

start

Fill in the missing **T** to complete the words.

 _ _ _ OP

 _ _ _ IGER

 _ _ _ REE

 _ _ _ OMATO

 _ _ _ RIANGLE

69

Lowercase Letter t

Trace the lowercase letter **t**.
Then try writing it on your own.

start

Color each truck with an uppercase **T** blue
and each truck with a lowercase **t** green.

Beginning Sounds

Say the word **t**oad.  **T**oad starts with the **T** sound. Say the name of each picture. Circle all of the pictures that begin with the **T** sound.

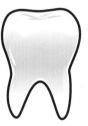

Uppercase Letter U

U is for _____MBRELLA.  Trace the uppercase letter **U**.
Then try writing it on your own.

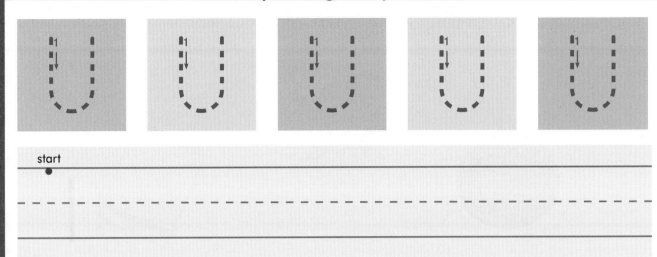

start

Find and circle all of the uppercase **U**'s in the large **U**.

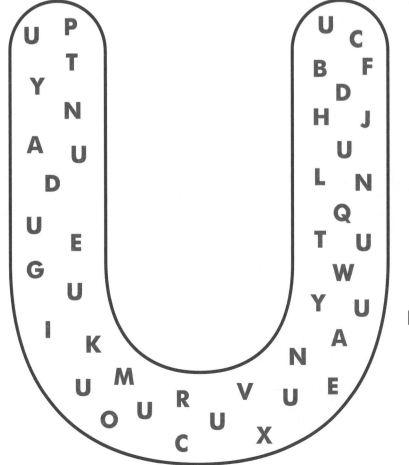

How many **U**'s did you find?

Lowercase Letter u

Trace the lowercase letter **u**.
Then try writing it on your own.

 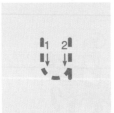 

start

Color anything with an uppercase **U** red  and anything with a lowercase **u** blue to see the hidden picture!

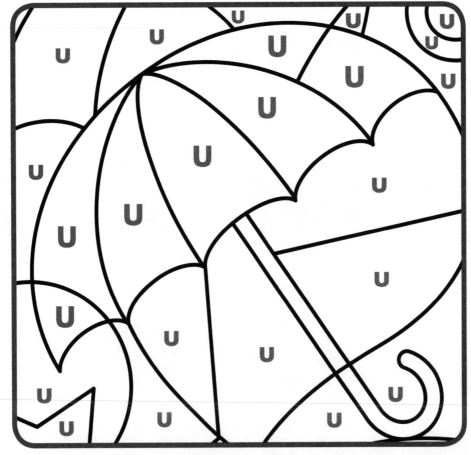

73

Beginning Sounds

Say the name of each picture. Circle the picture that begins with the sound of the letter in each row.

Qq

Rr

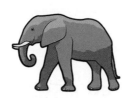 

Ss

Tt

Uu

Uppercase Letter V

V is for _____**IOLIN**.  Trace the uppercase letter **V**.
Then try writing it on your own.

start

Color all of the uppercase **V**'s.

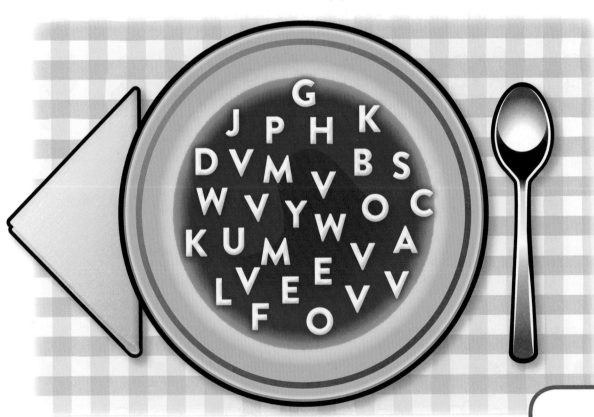

How many **V**'s
did you find?

75

Lowercase Letter v

Trace the lowercase letter **v**.
Then try writing it on your own.

start

Draw a line from each of the uppercase letter **V**'s to
one of the lowercase letter **v**'s in the violets below.

 V W M V U V

w v v m u v

Beginning Sounds

Say the name of each picture. Draw a line to the letter
that shows the beginning sound. Trace the letter.

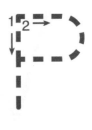

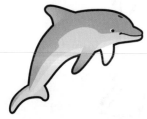

Uppercase Letter W

W is for _____AGON. 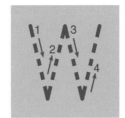 Trace the uppercase letter **W**.
Then try writing it on your own.

  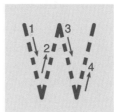 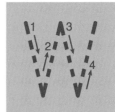

start

W is for **WOLF**. Color the **W**. Color the wolf.

Lowercase Letter w

Trace the lowercase letter **w**.
Then try writing it on your own.

start

Color all of the **w**hales that have a lowercase **w** in them.

Beginning Sounds

Say the name of each picture. Write an uppercase letter **S** next to each picture that starts with an **S** sound and an uppercase letter **W** next to each picture that begins with the **W** sound. If it does not begin with an **S** or a **W**, leave it blank.

Uppercase Letter X

X is for _____-**RAY**. 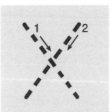 Trace the uppercase letter **X**.
Then try writing it on your own.

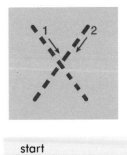 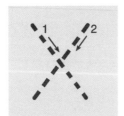 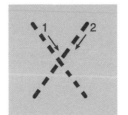 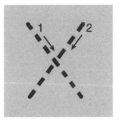

start

Find and circle all of the uppercase **X**'s in the large **X**.

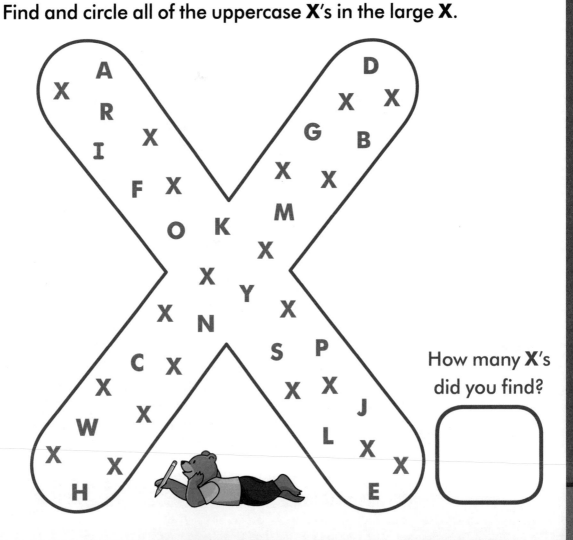

How many **X**'s
did you find?

Lowercase Letter x

Trace the lowercase letter **x**.
Then try writing it on your own.

start

Help the doctor **x**-ray his patient by showing
him the way through the maze.

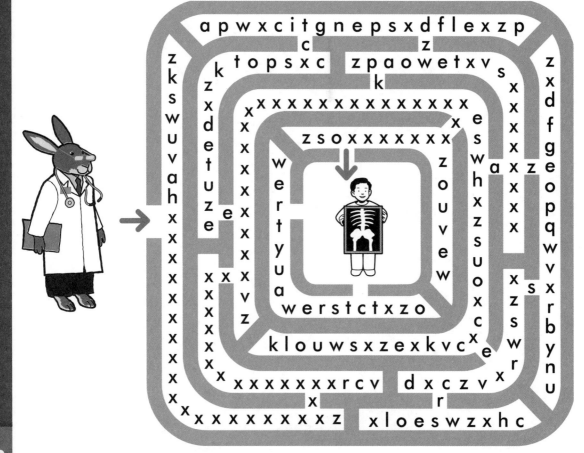

Ending Sounds

Write the missing letter for the ending sound.

x	l	f	r	k	r

fo _____

wol _____

dee _____

skun _____

squirre _____

bea _____

Uppercase Letter Y

Y is for _____O-YO. Trace the uppercase letter **Y**.
Then try writing it on your own.

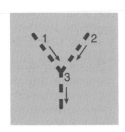  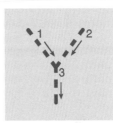 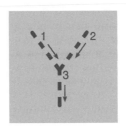 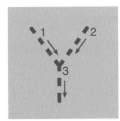

start

Color the pictures that begin with the letter **Y**.
Then add the letter **Y** to complete the word.

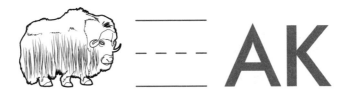 AK

 ARN

ELLOW

 OGURT

Lowercase Letter y

Trace the lowercase letter **y**.
Then try writing it on your own.

start

Draw a line from each uppercase **Y** to a lowercase **y** below.

Beginning Sounds

Say the name of each picture. Circle the picture that begins with the sound of the letter in each row.

Kk			
Ll			
Mm			
Nn			
Oo			
Pp			

Uppercase Letter Z

Z is for _____**EBRA**. 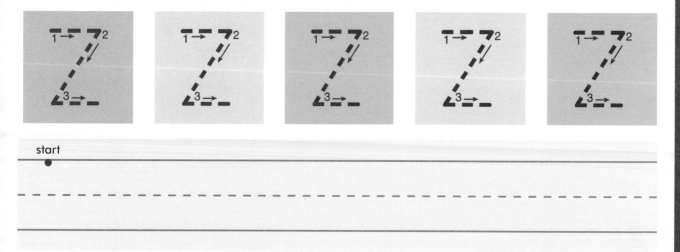 Trace the uppercase letter **Z**. Then try writing it on your own.

start

Find and circle all of the uppercase **Z**'s hidden at the **zoo**.

How many **Z**'s did you find?

Lowercase Letter z

Trace the lowercase letter **z**.
Then try writing it on your own.

start

Zippy the **Z**ebra loves to sleep!
Trace the **z**'s above his head so he can
get a good night's sleep.

Tall, Small, and Fall Letters

Trace the tall, small, and fall letters.

Tall Letters

b d f

h k l t

Small Letters

a c e i m

n o r s u

v w x z

Fall Letters

g j

p q y

89

SIGHT WORDS

red get

am ran say

Sight Word: AM

Read and Color It

I am at school.

Trace and Write It

_____   _____

am

Find and Circle It

am	in	are	all
all	am	at	am
is	as	am	an

Find and Color It

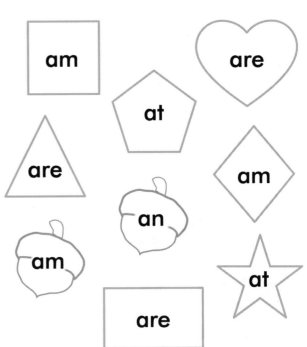

am   are

at

are   am

an

am

at

are

Box It: Tall, Small, or Fall?

Sight Word: WITH

SIGHT WORDS

Read and Color It

I will draw with you.

 **Trace and Write It**

Find and Circle It

with	why	will	with
what	will	with	we
win	with	was	won

Find and Color It

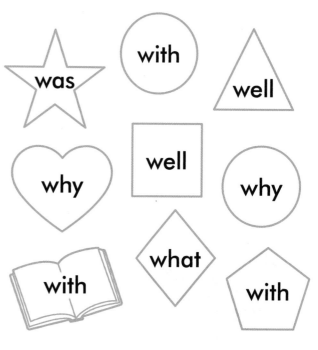

was

with

well

why

well

why

with

what

with

Box It: Tall, Small, or Fall?

Sight Word: ARE

Read and Color It

We **are** on a farm.

Trace and Write It

Find and Color It

are

at

are

all

art

are

ask

are

and

Find and Circle It

all	ant	and	ask
am	are	at	are
are	at	all	and

Box It: Tall, Small, or Fall?

Sight Word: AT

Read and Color It

We had fun at the party.

Trace and Write It

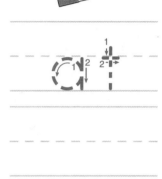

Find and Color It

at

at

at

at

as

an

at

it

am

Find and Circle It

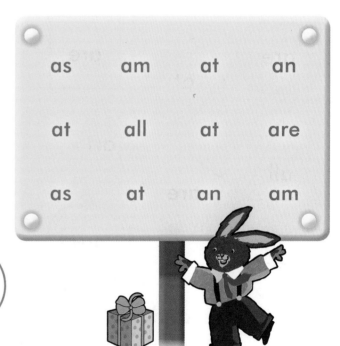

as	am	at	an
at	all	at	are
as	at	an	am

Box It: Tall, Small, or Fall?

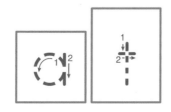

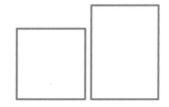

Sight Word: RAN

Read and Color It

I ran very fast.

 Trace and Write It

Find and Circle It

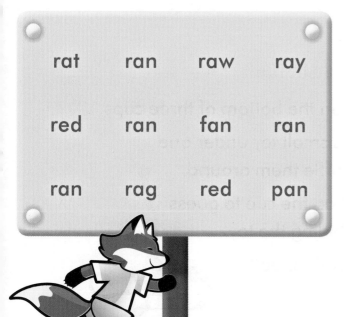

rat	ran	raw	ray
red	ran	fan	ran
ran	rag	red	pan

Find and Color It

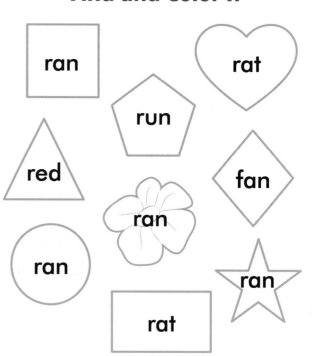

ran

rat

run

red

fan

ran

ran

ran

rat

Box It: Tall, Small, or Fall?

Sight Words

Sight Word of the Day!

Sing the song below using any sight word to the tune of "B-I-N-G-O."

Sight Word Song

There was a sight word for the day

and **like** was our sight word!

L – i – k – e, l – i – k – e, l – i – k – e,

and **like** was our sight word!

Sight Word Shuffle

Write a different sight word on the bottom of three cups.

Have someone hide a small toy under one of the cups and shuffle them around.

Read the sight word on the cup to guess which one is hiding the toy.

Have fun and repeat!

was   were   like

Sight Word: GET

Read and Color It

Go get the ball.

 Trace and Write It

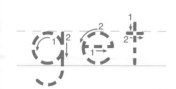

Find and Circle It

get	gas	got	get
let	get	gap	go
gum	gas	get	met

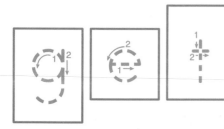

Find and Color It

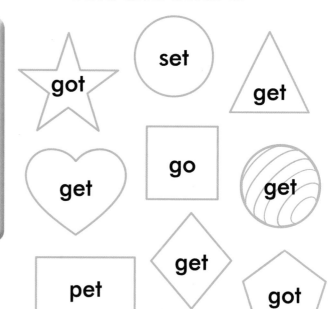

got   set   get   get   go   get   pet   get   got

Box It: Tall, Small, or Fall?

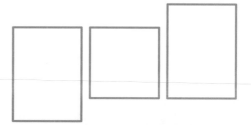

97

Sight Word: DID

Read and Color It

Did you go to the park?

Trace and Write It

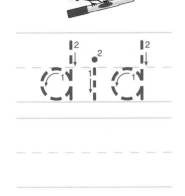

Find and Color It

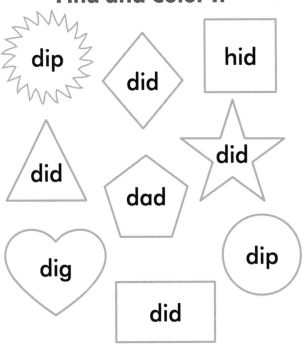

dip

did

hid

did

did

dad

dig

dip

did

Find and Circle It

day	hid	bed	did
dig	did	dad	had
did	dot	dog	did

Box It: Tall, Small, or Fall?

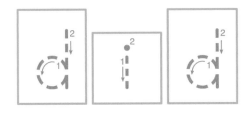

Sight Word: CAME

Read and Color It

I'm glad the sun came out!

Trace and Write It

Find and Circle It

come	came	call	card
came	cake	game	came
come	some	came	call

Find and Color It

came

card

same

card

game

came

same

come

came

Box It: Tall, Small, or Fall?

99

Read and Color It

Do you want milk?

Trace and Write It

Find and Circle It

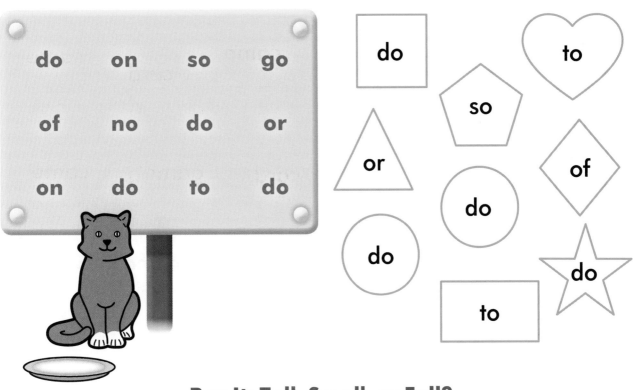

do	on	so	go
of	no	do	or
on	do	to	do

Find and Color It

do

to

so

or

of

do

do

do

to

Box It: Tall, Small, or Fall?

Sight Word: EAT

Read and Color It

I love to eat ice cream!

 **Trace and Write It**

Find and Circle It

elf	eat	egg	are
eat	end	eat	ate
egg	ate	eat	ear

Find and Color It

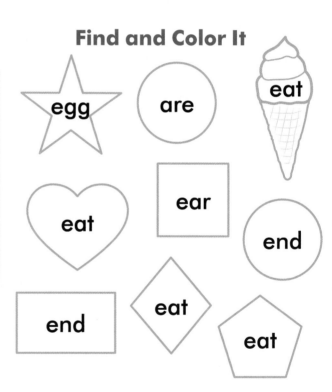

egg   are   eat

eat   ear   end

end   eat   eat

Box It: Tall, Small, or Fall?

  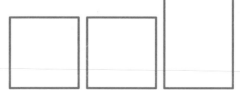

Sight Words

Sight Words Riddle

Color the picture to solve the riddle.

with = 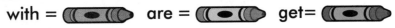   are =   get=

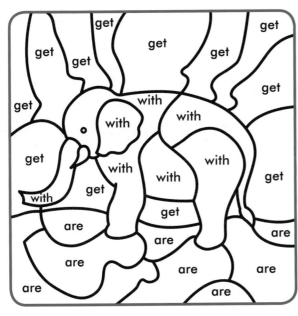

Who Am I?

I'm an animal you might love,

But I'm too big to be your pet.

I have an extremely long trunk,

And it's said I never forget.

Sight Word Target Practice

Write different sight words on a bunch of paper plates.

Tape the plates to the wall at different heights.

Call out the word you are going to hit and then
throw a soft ball at the plate to try and hit it.

Play by yourself or with a friend.

Sight Word: SAY

Read and Color It

What does a dog say?

Trace and Write It

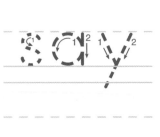

Find and Color It

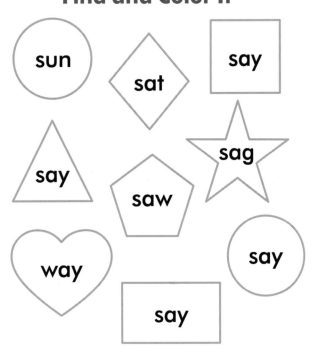

sun

sat

say

say

sag

saw

way

say

say

Find and Circle It

sat	sad	see	say
saw	say	hay	ray
say	sit	sun	say

Box It: Tall, Small, or Fall?

Sight Word: GOOD

Read and Color It

Fruit is good for you!

Trace and Write It

Find and Circle It

give	good	gold	good
good	gone	gray	glad
game	good	grab	good

Find and Color It

good

give

good

gone

 good

food

gold

grab

 good

Box It: Tall, Small, or Fall?

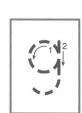    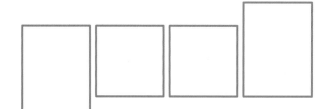

Sight Word: HAVE

Read and Color It

May I have some candy?

Trace and Write It

Find and Circle It

hoot	have	hall	have
have	hike	hard	gave
home	help	have	save

Find and Color It

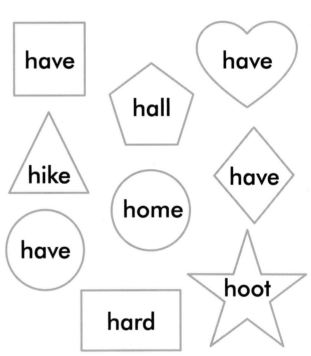

have   have

hall

hike   have

home

have

hoot

hard

Box It: Tall, Small, or Fall?

Sight Word: HE

Read and Color It

He likes to play ball.

Trace and Write It

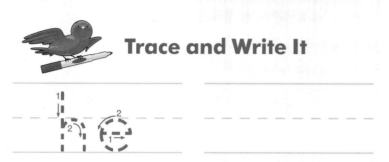

Find and Circle It

he	hi	me	her
he	be	he	be
by	she	we	he

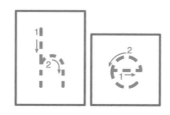

Find and Color It

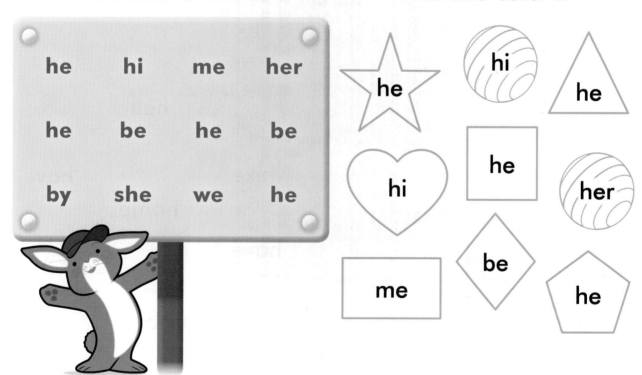

he hi he
hi he her
me be he

Box It: Tall, Small, or Fall?

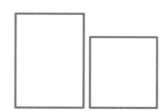

Sight Word: INTO

Read and Color It

The pig fell into the mud.

Trace and Write It

Find and Circle It

into	onto	ice	into
onto	into	igloo	inch
inch	inside	info	into

Find and Color It

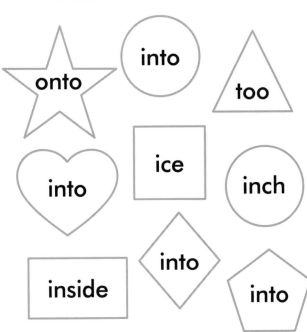

onto
into
too
ice
inch
into
inside
into
into

Box It: Tall, Small, or Fall?

107

Sight Words

Sight Word Tic-Tac-Toe

Play tic-tac-toe with a friend. First read the sight words, then cross each one off with an X or an O.

did	came	do
eat	say	good
have	he	into

am	with	ran
are	at	get
was	were	like

were	with	say
did	ran	have
do	get	into

are	like	good
at	did	have
ran	came	he

get	do	into
am	was	eat
with	were	say

at	did	have
eat	do	ran
were	say	eat

Sight Word Hopscotch

Draw a hopscotch board with chalk.

Write a different sight word in each box.

When you throw the rock on a box, you must read the sight word in it.

Play until all the sight words have been read.

Have fun hopping!

108

Sight Word: LIKE

Read and Color It

Do you like pizza?

Trace and Write It

Find and Color It

like

lick

love

lake

like

like

bike

like

Find and Circle It

line	like	lake	like
lime	bike	like	late
leaf	like	lift	lion

Box It: Tall, Small, or Fall?

Sight Word: NEW

Read and Color It

This is my new bike.

Trace and Write It

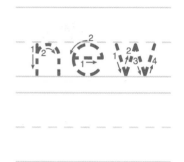

new

Find and Color It

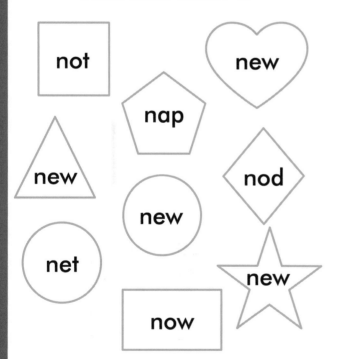

not

new

nap

new

nod

new

net

new

now

Find and Circle It

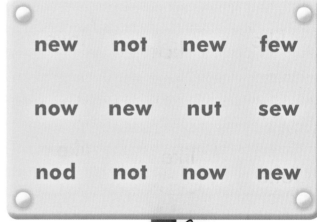

new	not	new	few
now	new	nut	sew
nod	not	now	new

Box It: Tall, Small, or Fall?

   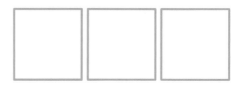

Sight Word: WILL

Read and Color It

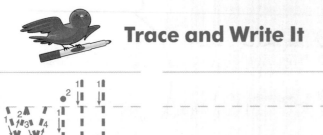 **Will** you come to my party?

Trace and Write It

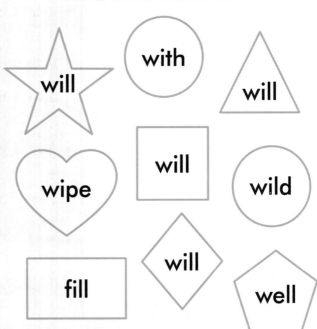

Find and Circle It

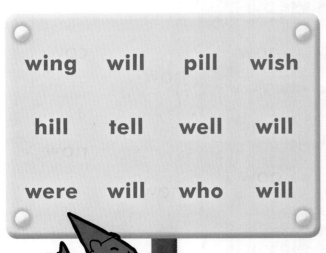

wing	will	pill	wish
hill	tell	well	will
were	will	who	will

Find and Color It

will   with   will

wipe   will   wild

fill   will   well

Box It: Tall, Small, or Fall?

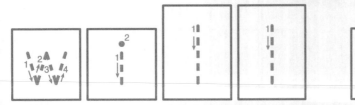

Sight Word: NOW

Read and Color It

Please feed your fish now.

 **Trace and Write It**

Find and Circle It

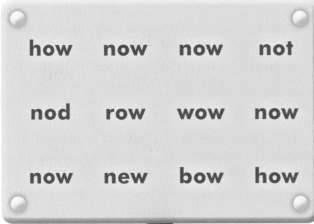

how	now	now	not
nod	row	wow	now
now	new	bow	how

Find and Color It

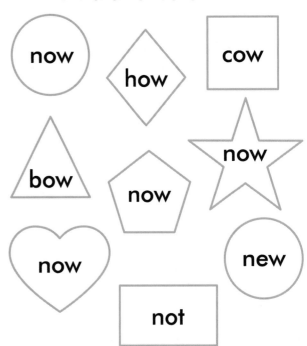

now

how

cow

bow

now

now

now

new

not

Box It: Tall, Small, or Fall?

Sight Word: ON

Read and Color It

I rode on my scooter.

Trace and Write It

Find and Color It

no

on

in

as

on

of

on

on

on

Find and Circle It

on	in	on	of
no	on	oh	on
an	is	at	or

Box It: Tall, Small, or Fall?

113

I Can Read

Underline the words she, he, and they in the sentences below.

She is a girl.

She is happy.

He is a boy.

He is sad.

They are friends.

Now he is happy!

Sight Word: MUST

Read and Color It

You must brush your teeth.

Trace and Write It

Find and Circle It

much	rest	most	must
must	nest	must	mist
dust	must	more	test

Find and Color It

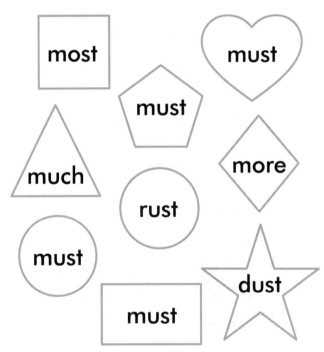

most

must

must

much

more

rust

must

dust

must

Box It: Tall, Small, or Fall?

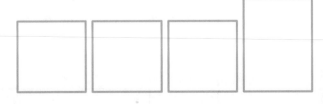

Sight Word: PLEASE

Read and Color It

Please read me a book.

Trace and Write It

Find and Circle It

choose	excuse	praise
people	please	these
please	refuse	please
please	house	player

Find and Color It

please

please

plates

planet

cheese

plants

please

please

Box It: Tall, Small, or Fall?

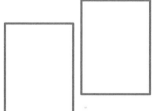

116

Sight Word: PRETTY

Read and Color It

The flower is so pretty.

Trace and Write It

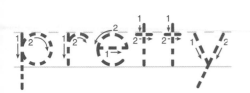

Find and Circle It

plenty	pretty	sporty
prizes	prince	pretty
party	pretty	safety
happy	please	pretty

Find and Color It

party

twenty

party

pretty

pretty

really

pretty

pretty

Box It: Tall, Small, or Fall?

Sight Word: SAW

Read and Color It

I saw a fire truck.

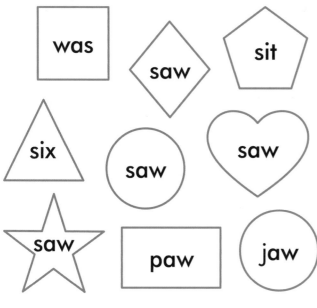

Trace and Write It

Find and Color It

was

saw

sit

six

saw

saw

saw

paw

jaw

Find and Circle It

saw	sad	saw	was
say	see	sat	saw
jaw	paw	saw	sit

Box It: Tall, Small, or Fall?

Sight Word: RIDE

Read and Color It

I like to ride in a boat.

Trace and Write It

Find and Circle It

ride	rode	ripe	ride
rain	ride	rest	rock
rice	tide	ride	side

Find and Color It

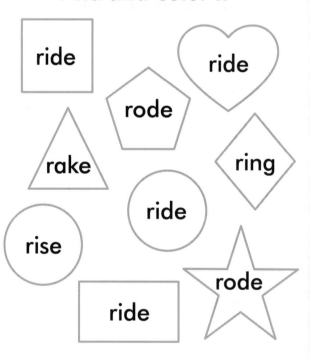

ride   ride
rode
rake   ring
ride
rise   rode
ride

Box It: Tall, Small, or Fall?

Sight Word: WENT

Read and Color It

I went to the store.

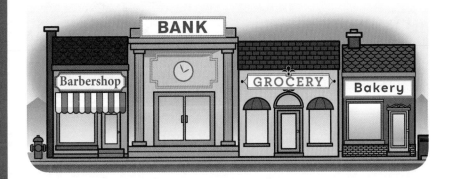

Trace and Write It

Find and Color It

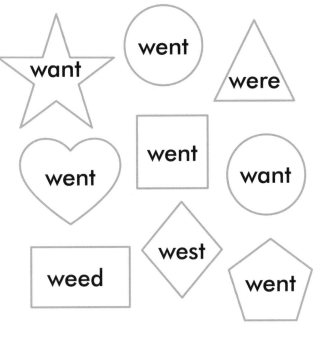

want

went

were

went

went

want

weed

west

went

Find and Circle It

want	went	walk	tent
were	went	bent	went
week	will	went	sent

Box It: Tall, Small, or Fall?

Sight Words

Sight Words Riddle

Color the picture to solve the riddle.

yes = ![crayon] our = ![crayon] out= ![crayon] on= ![crayon]

Who Am I?

If you go on safari, this creature's hard to ignore.
Because he is king and he has a mighty roar!

Sight Word Dot Art

Use Q-tips for brushes with four different colors of paint.

On a blank piece of paper, paint dots to spell out your favorite sight word.

Fill in the rest of the page with dots so it is covered in color.

Sight Word: SHE

Read and Color It

She likes the beach.

Trace and Write It

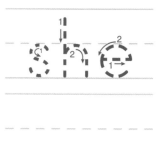

Find and Color It

she

he

shh

see

she

she

she

she

shy

she

Find and Circle It

the	saw	shy	she
say	she	sea	her
sky	see	she	she

Box It: Tall, Small, or Fall?

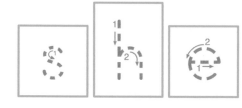

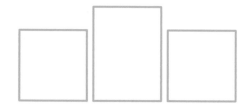

122

Sight Word: WHO

Read and Color It

Who wants cake?

Trace and Write It

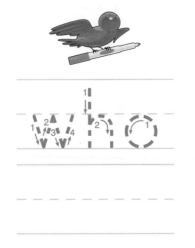

Find and Color It

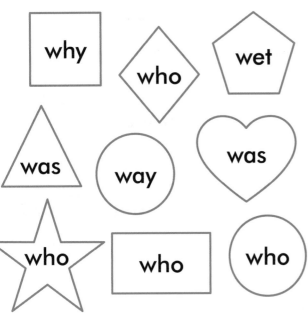

why

who

wet

was

way

was

who

who

who

Find and Circle It

was	why	how	who
who	wet	who	web
was	who	wow	wet

Box It: Tall, Small, or Fall?

Sight Word: UNDER

Read and Color It

The apples were under the tree.

Trace and Write It

Find and Circle It

uncle	unzip	under	over
rider	under	wider	under
under	upper	until	order

Find and Color It

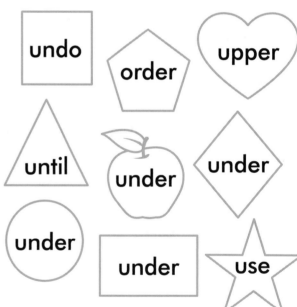

undo

order

upper

until

under

under

under

under

use

Box It: Tall, Small, or Fall?

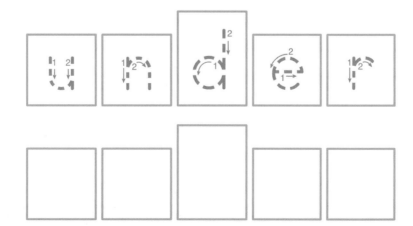

Sight Word: THAT

Read and Color It

That balloon is blue.

Trace and Write It

Find and Circle It

that	this	what	that
flat	them	that	then
they	that	coat	them

Find and Color It

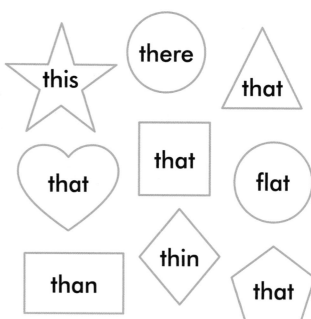

this

there

that

that

that

flat

than

thin

that

Box It: Tall, Small, or Fall?

Sight Word: BUT

Read and Color It

I like baseball but my friend likes basketball.

Trace and Write It

Find and Color It

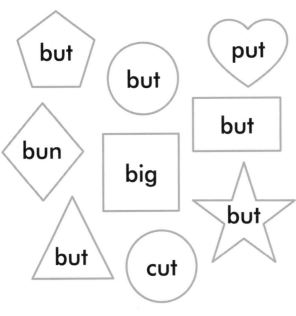

but

but

put

bun

big

but

but

but

cut

Find and Circle It

bad	but	bat	out
but	boy	bus	put
cut	big	but	but

Box It: Tall, Small, or Fall?

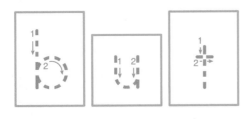

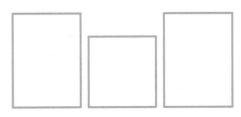

Sight Words

Sight Word Rainbow

Find the following sight words and color the band.

yes = (crayon)   was = (crayon)   no = (crayon)

our = (crayon)   want = (crayon)   too = (crayon)

yes

was

no

want

too

yes

yes

our

too

too

too

too

too

too

too

too

yes

too

yes

yes

too

too

too

Sight Word Memory

Have an adult cut about 24 small squares of paper for you.

Write the same sight word on two squares until all of the squares are filled.

Turn them all over so the blank side is up. Mix them and then play the game Memory!

Good luck!

Sight Word: THIS

Read and Color It

This is my pet cat Goldie.

Trace and Write It

Find and Circle It

this	this	that	there
then	his	this	thin
here	this	then	them

Find and Color It

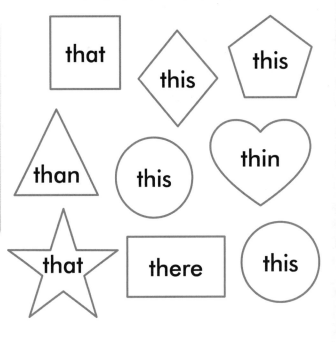

that

this

this

than

this

thin

that

there

this

Box It: Tall, Small, or Fall?

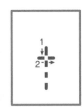   

Sight Word: TOO

Read and Color It

I like to play ball too.

 **Trace and Write It**

Find and Circle It

toy	boo	too	two
toe	too	zoo	the
too	moo	ton	too

Find and Color It

boo

too

too

too

top

too

toe

too

toy

Box It: Tall, Small, or Fall?

 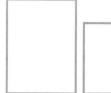 

Sight Word: SOON

Read and Color It

Soon it will be winter.

 **Trace and Write It**

Find and Circle It

some	moon	soon	noon
some	soon	food	soon
soon	room	some	moon

Find and Color It

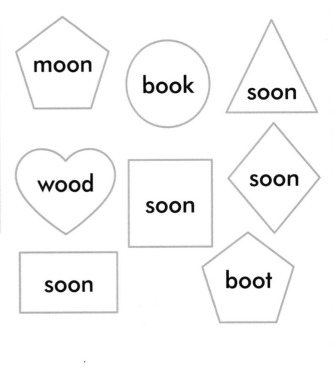

moon   book   soon

wood   soon   soon

soon   boot

Box It: Tall, Small, or Fall?

SIGHT WORDS

Sight Word: WANT

Read and Color It

Do you want to play?

Trace and Write It

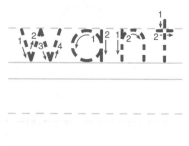

Find and Color It

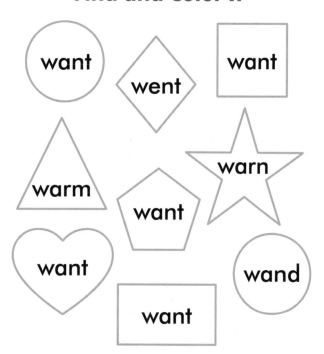

want

went

want

warm

warn

want

want

wand

want

Find and Circle It

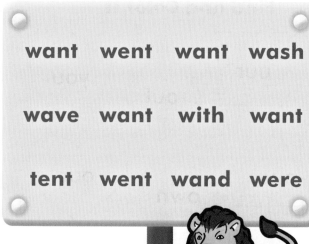

want	went	want	wash
wave	want	with	want
tent	went	wand	were

Box It: Tall, Small, or Fall?

Sight Word: OUR

Read and Color It

This is our house.

Trace and Write It

Find and Color It

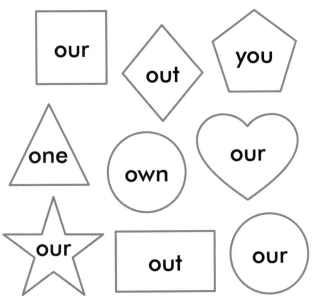

our

out

you

one

own

our

our

out

our

Find and Circle It

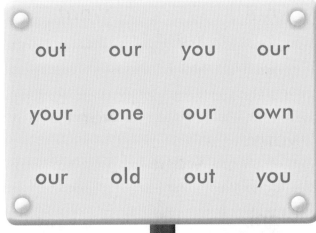

out	our	you	our
your	one	our	own
our	old	out	you

Box It: Tall, Small, or Fall?

132

Sight Words

Sight Words Riddle

Color the picture to solve the riddle.

am = 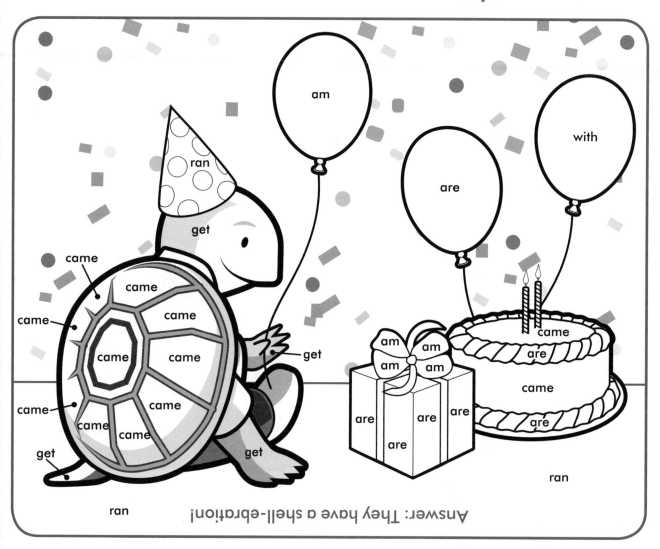   are =   ran =
get =   came =   with =

What do turtles do for their birthday?

Answer: They have a shell-ebration!

Flashlight Hide and Seek

Write ten different sight words on pieces of paper. Ask an adult to tape them up in a dark room. Turn out the lights and try to find the sight words with a flashlight. Yell out the word when you find it.

Sight Word: NO

Read and Color It

No, I do not like snakes.

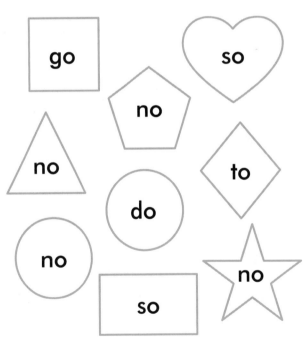

Trace and Write It

no

Find and Circle It

go	no	so	to
no	on	no	or
go	of	on	no

Find and Color It

go

so

no

no

to

do

no

so

no

Box It: Tall, Small, or Fall?

Sight Word: OUT

Read and Color It

Let's play out in the rain.

Trace and Write It

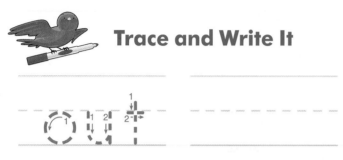

Find and Circle It

our	out	one	but
nut	out	put	out
our	one	out	old

Find and Color It

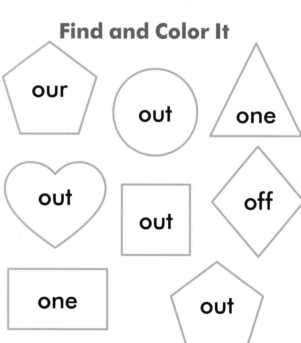

our

out

one

out

out

off

one

out

Box It: Tall, Small, or Fall?

135

Sight Word: YES

Read and Color It

Yes, it is my birthday.

Trace and Write It

Find and Color It

yes

you

yet

yum

way

yes

yes

yes

hey

Find and Circle It

you	yes	hey	yes
yes	yet	set	way
you	day	yes	say

Box It: Tall, Small, or Fall?

Sight Word: THERE

Read and Color It

There is a circus coming to town.

 ## Trace and Write It

Find and Circle It

there	those	thank
thing	there	threw
three	them	there
thumb	there	thing

Find and Color It

these

think

there

there

that

there

threw

there

their

Box It: Tall, Small, or Fall?

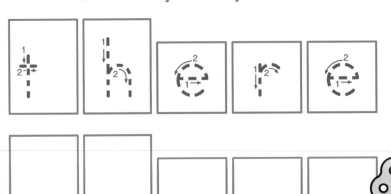

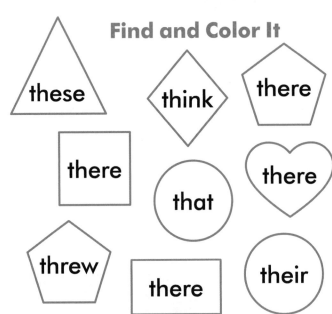

137

Sight Words: WAS

Read and Color It

The child was in a car.

Trace and Write It

Find and Circle It

was	win	saw	was
way	was	was	web
why	saw	wet	wax

Find and Color It

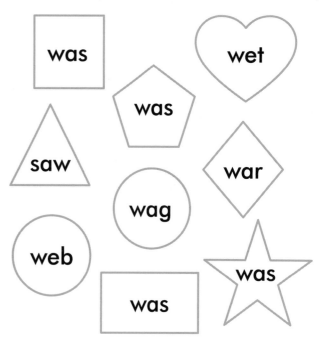

was · wet · was · saw · war · wag · web · was · was

Box It: Tall, Small, or Fall?

Read and Color It

They are a family.

Trace and Write It

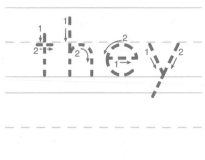

Find and Color It

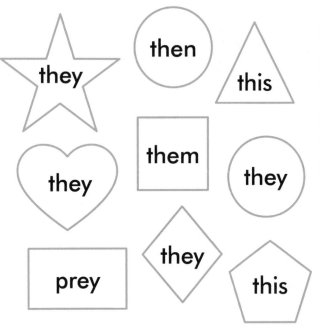

they

then

this

they

them

they

prey

they

this

Find and Circle It

that	tray	they	this
they	thin	here	then
stay	they	them	they

Box It: Tall, Small, or Fall?

SIZES, COMPARISONS & OPPOSITES

Same Size

Look at the pictures of vegetables in each row.
Circle the picture of the vegetable in each row that
is the **same size** as the picture at the left.

Draw a triangle in the box the exact
same size as the orange triangle.

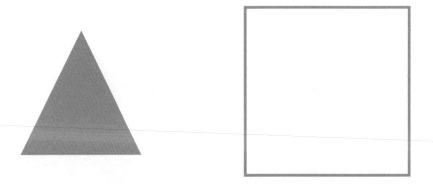

Different Size

Look at the picture of the bugs in each row.
Circle the picture of the bug in each row that
is a **different size** than the picture at the left.

Bigger and Smaller

Look at the musical instruments in each box.
Color the one that is **bigger**.

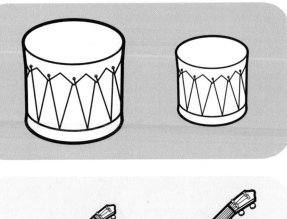

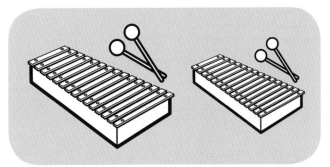

Look at the musical instruments in each box.
Color the one that is **smaller**.

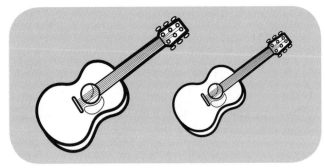

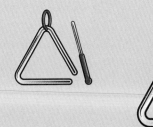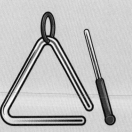

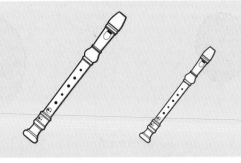

Bigger and Smaller

Number the items 1, 2, or 3 from **smallest** to **biggest**.

   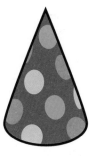

Slower or Faster

A turtle is **slow**.
A turtle is **slower** than a rabbit.

A rabbit is **fast**.
A rabbit is **faster** than a turtle.

Circle the correct answer.

panther   cat

A panther is **slower faster**
than a cat.

deer   cow

A deer is **slower faster** than
a cow.

crab   shark

A crab is **slower faster** than
a shark.

frog   worm

A frog is **slower faster** than a
worm.

Left or Right

Trace the words **left** and **right** below. Now look at your hands and say which one is **left** and which one is **right**.

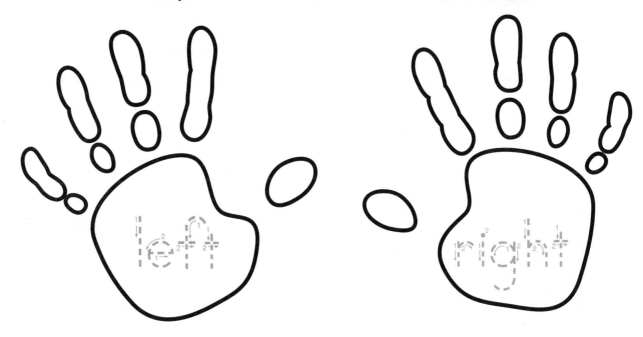

Color the birds on the **left** side of the tree **red**.
Color the birds on the **right** side of the tree **blue**.

What Goes Together?

Look at the pictures in each row. Three of the items go together and one does not. Draw an **X** over the item that does **not** go with the rest.

147

What Goes Together?

Draw a line from the things in the top row that go together with those in the bottom row.

Draw something in the box below that goes with a barn.

Find the Pattern

Look at the patterns below. Circle **yes** if the patterns are the same. Circle **no** if the patterns are different.

Are these patterns the same?   Yes   No

Are these patterns the same?   Yes   No

Are these patterns the same?   Yes   No

SIZES, COMPARISONS & OPPOSITES

Find the Match

All the snowmen are different except for two.
Find the match. Circle the two snowmen
that are exactly **the same**.

Words That Rhyme

Draw a line from each word on the left
to the word that **rhymes** with it on the right.

lock

phone

cat

star

bone

mouse

car

clock

house

hat

Words That Rhyme

Draw a line from each word on the left to the word that **rhymes** with it on the right.

corn

can

school

wig

pig

kite

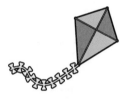

light

pool

van

horn

Same Size

Circle the picture of the animal in each row that is the **same size** as the picture at the left.

Draw a circle in the box below the exact **same size** as the purple circle.

Different Size

Circle the picture of the animal in each row that is a **different size** than the picture at the left.

Top, Middle & Bottom

Color the top light **red**, which means stop.
Color the middle light **yellow**, which means caution.
Color the bottom light **green**, which means go.

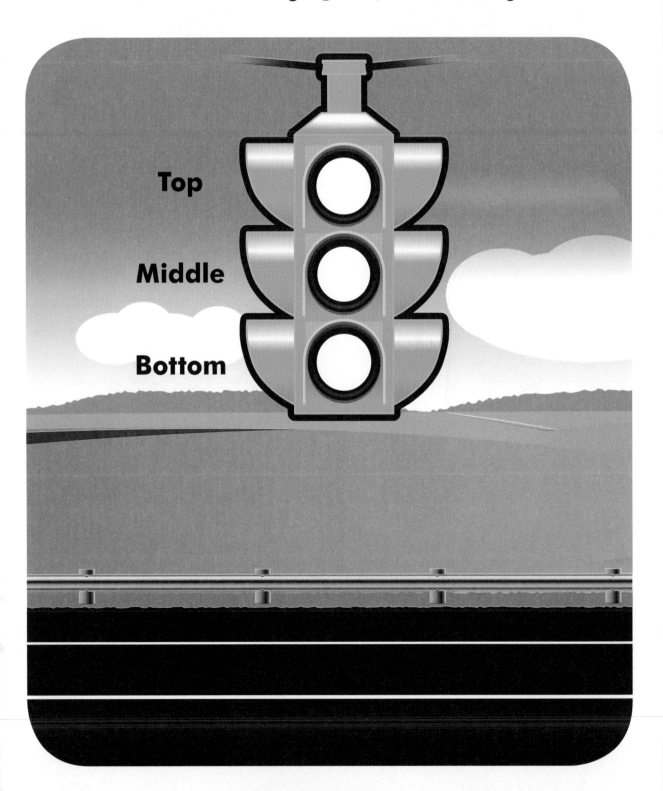

Top

Middle

Bottom

Shorter & Taller

Put an **X** under the **shorter** tree.

Color the **taller** animal below.

Complete the sentence with either **short** or **tall**.

 He is   short   tall.   She is   short   tall.

In & Out

Trace the words **in** and **out**.

Write **in** or **out** in the following sentences.

The  is _____ the mailbox.

The 🕷 is _____ of the web.

The 🐿 is _____ the tree.

The 🦆 is _____ of the water.

SIZES, COMPARISONS & OPPOSITES

Up & Down

Circle **up** or **down** in the following sentences.

The bear is   **up**   **down**   on the seesaw.

The fox is   **up**   **down**   on the seesaw.

The turtle swims

up   **down**.

The turtle swims

up   **down**.

Opposites

Look carefully at the pictures and draw a line connecting each word to its **opposite**.

 asleep

cold

 slow

strong

 happy

awake

 weak

fast

 open

sad

 hot

closed

Opposites

Look carefully at the pictures and draw a line connecting each word to its **opposite**.

 clean

night

 short

back

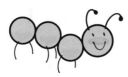 day

full

 front

dirty

 empty

long

Patterns

Look at the pictures below. There is a **pattern** in each row.
Once you have figured out the **pattern**, circle what comes next.

 or

 or

 or

 or

Help the crab get to the ocean by following the
shape pattern triangle ▲, circle ●, square ■, in the maze below.

SIZES, COMPARISONS & OPPOSITES

Find the Pattern

Look at the **patterns** in each column, running top to bottom.
Circle **yes** if the **patterns** are the same.
Circle **no** if the **patterns** are different.

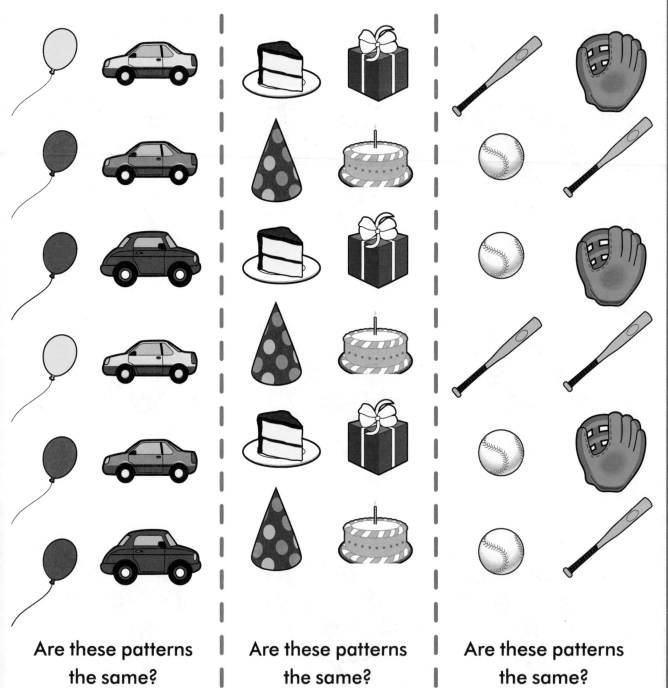

Are these patterns
the same?

Yes   No

Are these patterns
the same?

Yes   No

Are these patterns
the same?

Yes   No

Find the Match

All the ladybugs are different except for two.
Find the match. Circle the two ladybugs
that are exactly **the same**.

Words That Rhyme

Draw a line from each word on the left to the word that **rhymes** with it on the right.

block

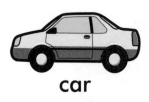

car

nail

kittens

star

mail

snake

sock

mittens

rake

Draw a line from each word on the left to the
word that **rhymes** with it on the right.

 rug

fruit

 sun

fun

 dish

bug

 ball

tall

 suit

fish

Same Size

Look at the pictures in each box.
Circle the pictures that are the **same size**.

Bigger and Smaller

In each row, draw an **X** through the **biggest** animal and **circle** the **smallest** animal.

Wet or Dry?

Look at the picture and then circle whether the animal lives in a **wet** or a **dry** environment.

wet   dry

wet   dry

wet   dry

wet   dry

wet   dry

wet   dry

Hot or Cold?

Draw a line from each picture to the thermometer that is either **cold** or **hot**.

Over and Under

Trace the words **over** and **under** and then write them on your own.

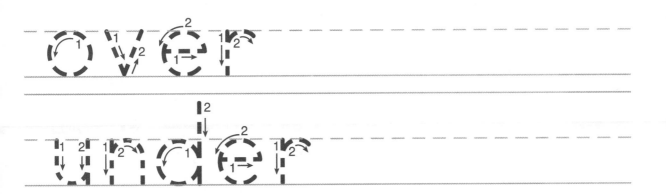

The bee is **over** the flower.

The worm is **under** the flower.

Color the spider **over** the web **black**.
Color the spider **under** the web **brown**.

Full or Empty?

Look at each picture. Draw a line from the **full** box to each of the items that are **full**. Then draw a line from the **empty** box to each of the items that are **empty**.

FULL

EMPTY

Patterns

Look at the pictures below.
There is a pattern in each row, running from top to bottom.
Once you have figured out the pattern, circle what comes next.

or   or   or   or

Shape Patterns

Help the cow get to the barn by following this **shape pattern** ● ■ ♥ in the maze below.

SIZES, COMPARISONS & OPPOSITES

What Goes Together?

Look at the pictures in each row. Three of the items go together and one does not. Draw an **X** over the item that does **not** go with the rest.

   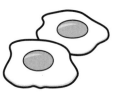

175

Draw a line from the object in the top row
that goes with the object in the bottom row.

Draw something in the box that goes with a scarf.

NUMBERS & COUNTING

1
2
3

1 One

Trace the number **1** and the word **one**.

How many ones do you count?

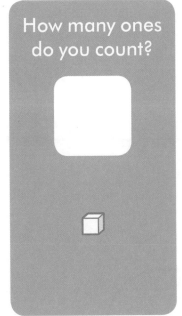

Count the planes and color the plane labeled number **1**.

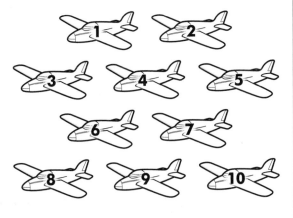

Circle all the number **1**'s.

1	2	1	3	9
				1
5	1	7	1	1
			8	
1		1		5
	6		2	1
3		1		1
	4		9	

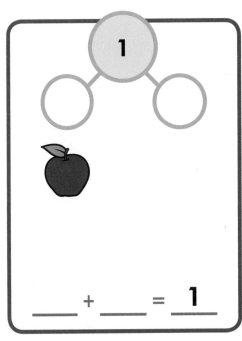

1

_____ + _____ = 1

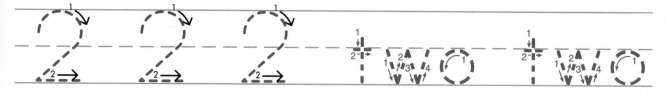

2 Two

Trace the number **2** and the word **two**.

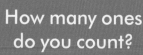

How many ones do you count?

Count the ants and color the ant labeled number **2**.

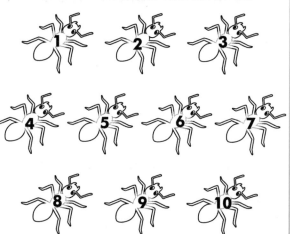

Circle all the number **2**'s.

1		6	5		4
	2			2	
2		8			
	6		3	5	9
9		2			
	4		8		2
		3		5	
2					7
	7		2		

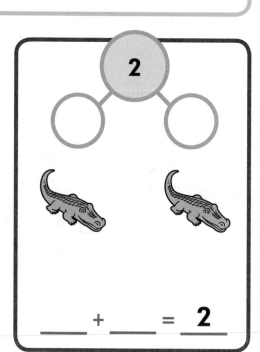

2

_____ + _____ = **2**

NUMBERS & COUNTING

Numbers

Tally marks are used to count or keep score. They are grouped in sets of five, which makes counting faster. Each | mark equals 1. After there are four | marks, a / mark crosses through them, which equals five.

1	I	6	⊬⊬ I
2	II	7	⊬⊬ II
3	III	8	⊬⊬ III
4	IIII	9	⊬⊬ IIII
5	⊬⊬	10	⊬⊬ ⊬⊬

Count the tally marks and circle the correct number.

| ||

1 2 3 4   1 2 3 4

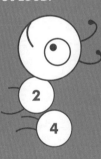

SKIP-COUNT BY
2's.

SAY THE NUMBERS OUT LOUD.

2
4

Circle the first tree. Draw a line under the second tree.

Color the robot with the smallest number.

  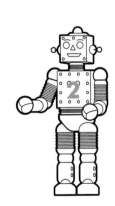

Write the smallest number.

_____

- - - - - - - - - -

_____

Write the largest number.

_____

- - - - - - - - - -

_____

COLOR NUMBERS 1 AND 2

Numbers

Count each group of shapes and add them together.
Write your answer on the line.

2 + 3 = _____

4 + 1 = _____

1 + 3 = _____

2 + 2 = _____

Greater Than or Less Than

Alligators are hungry animals. They always want to eat the bigger number. Think of the open end of the symbol < as the open mouth of an alligator trying to eat the bigger number.

 1 < 3   4 > 2

Now you try. Have the alligator eat the bigger number. Draw a < if the number on the right is bigger or a > if the number on the left is bigger. The first one is done for you.

3 (>) 1   1 ( ) 4   5 ( ) 2   3 ( ) 4

 10 11 12 13 14 15 16 17 18 19 20

3 Three

Trace the number **3** and the word **three**.

How many ones do you count?

Count the balloons and color the balloon labeled number **3**.

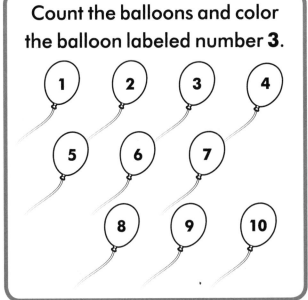

1 2 3 4

5 6 7

8 9 10

Circle all the number **3**'s.

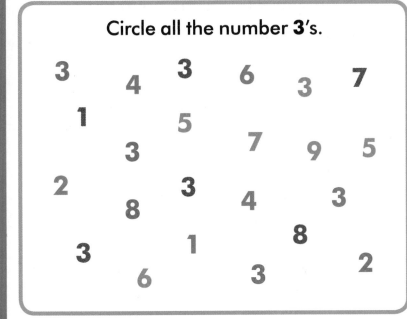

3 4 **3** 6 3 **7**

1 5

3 7 9 5

2 **3**

8 4 **3**

3 1 **8**

6 3 2

3

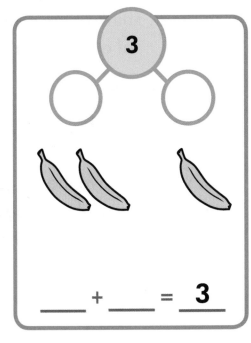

___ + ___ = **3**

4 Four

Trace the number **4** and the word **four**.

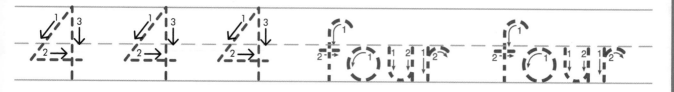

How many ones do you count?

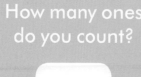

Count the bats and color the bat labeled number **4**.

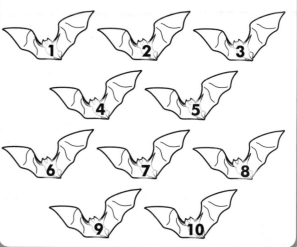

Circle all the number **4**'s.

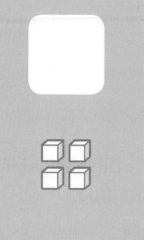

2   6   4   9
5   2
4   3
7   5   4   6
1   4
8   7   3
4   1
8   4
9   4

4

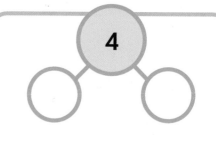

_____ + _____ = _____ 4

10 11 12 13 14 15 16 17 18 19 20

Numbers

Tally marks are used to count or keep score. They are grouped in sets of five, which makes counting faster. Each | mark equals 1. After there are four | marks, a / mark crosses through them, which equals five.

1	I	6	⊬ I
2	II	7	⊬ II
3	III	8	⊬ III
4	IIII	9	⊬ IIII
5	⊬	10	⊬ ⊬

Count the tally marks and circle the correct number.

||| ||||

1 2 3 4   1 2 3 4

Moving left to right, count the frogs. Circle the third frog. Draw a line under the fourth frog.

SKIP-COUNT BY
2's.
SAY THE NUMBERS OUT LOUD.

Circle the number of fish in each bowl.

1 2 3 4

1 2 3 4

1 2 3 4

1 2 3 4

COLOR NUMBERS 3 AND 4

Numbers

Look at the numbers in each row below and finish the pattern.

1   2   3   1   2 _____

3   4   3   4   3 _____

1   2   1   2   1 _____

Count each item and add them together. Write your answer on the line.

1 + 3 = _____

2 + 2 = _____

4 + 1 = _____

2 + 3 = _____

10 11 12 13 14 15 16 17 18 19 20

5 Five

Trace the number **5** and the word **five**.

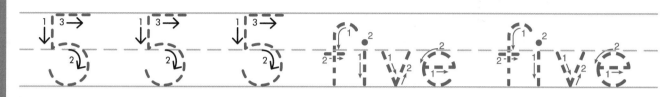

How many ones do you count?

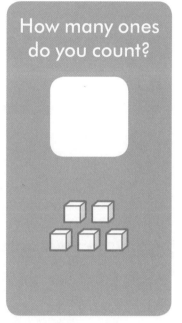

Count the pails and color the pail labeled number **5**.

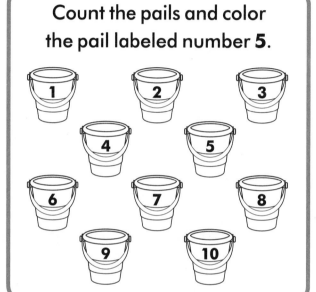

Circle all the number **5**'s.

5	3	6	2	9	5
1		4		
	5		5	9	4
8		8		2
	7		6	
5		3		5
	1		7	5

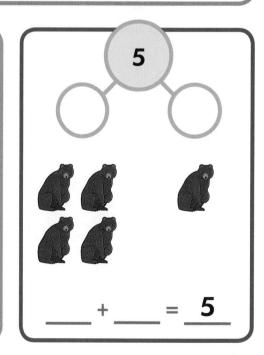

5

____ + ____ = __5__

 1 2 3 4 5 6 7 8 9

6 Six

Trace the number **6** and the word **six**.

How many ones do you count?

Count the hives and color the hive labeled number **6**.

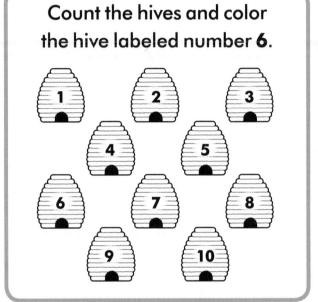

Circle all the number **6**'s.

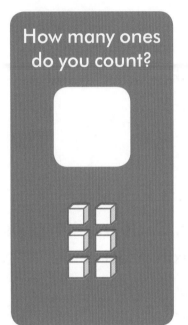

6

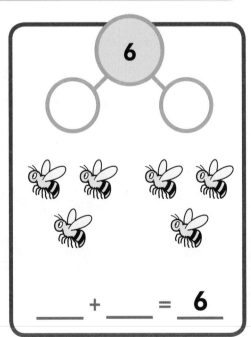

____ + ____ = **6**

Numbers

Tally marks are used to count or keep score. They are grouped in sets of five, which makes counting faster. Each | mark equals 1. After there are four | marks, a / mark crosses through them, which equals five.

1	I	6	IIII I
2	II	7	IIII II
3	III	8	IIII III
4	IIII	9	IIII IIII
5	IIII	10	IIII IIII

Count the tally marks and circle the correct number.

IIII

3　4　5　6

IIII I

3　4　5　6

SKIP-COUNT BY
2's.
SAY THE NUMBERS OUT LOUD.

Moving left to right, count the ghosts. Circle the fifth ghost. Draw a line under the sixth ghost.

2
4
6
8
10
12
14
16

Count the balls in each row. Draw a line to the matching number.

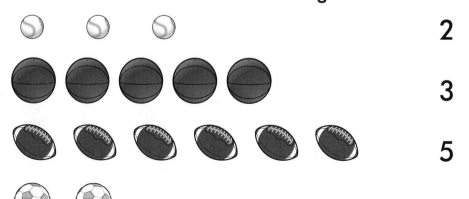

2

3

5

6

COLOR NUMBERS 5 AND 6

1　2　3　4　5　6　7　8　9

Numbers

Find the numbers in the word search below.
The words may run across or down.

ONE

TWO

THREE

FOUR

FIVE

Z	E	L	T	H	R	E	E	K	X
F	O	U	R	O	T	L	I	M	V
J	K	T	A	X	M	L	H	N	E
E	O	O	N	I	N	P	J	T	R
N	P	N	D	O	N	B	P	W	T
B	F	E	A	F	I	V	E	O	Y

Count each item and add them together. Write your answer on the line.

1 + 2 = _____

3 + 2 = _____

0 + 4 = _____

1 + 3 = _____

 10 11 12 13 14 15 16 17 18 19 20

189

7 Seven

Trace the number **7** and the word **seven**.

How many ones do you count?

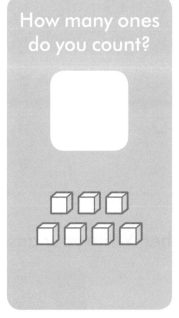

Count the birds and color the bird labeled number **7**.

Circle all the number **7**'s.

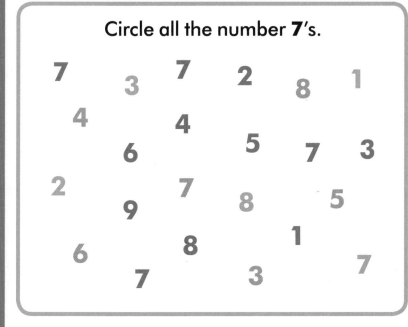

7		7	2		1
	3			8	
4		4			
	6		5	7	3
2		7			5
	9		8		
				1	
6		8			7
	7		3		

7

____ + ____ = **7**

8 Eight

Trace the number **8** and the word **eight**.

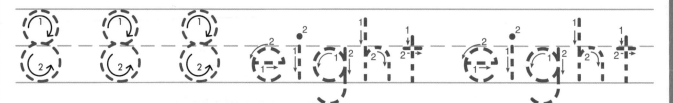

How many ones do you count?

Count the cakes and color the cake labeled number **8**.

Circle all the number **8**'s.

7   4   8   2   6

1

4   6

8   3   7   8

3   9

5   8   9

2

8   5   8

9   1

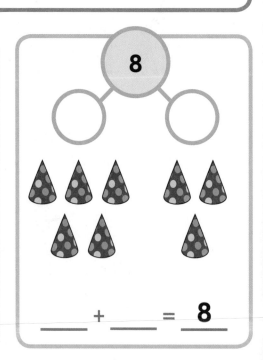

8

____ + ____ = **8**

Numbers

Tally marks are used to count or keep score. They are grouped in sets of five, which makes counting faster. Each | mark equals 1. After there are four | marks, a / mark crosses through them, which equals five.

1	I	6	⊁I
2	II	7	⊁II
3	III	8	⊁III
4	IIII	9	⊁IIII
5	⊁	10	⊁⊁

Count the tally marks and circle the correct number.

⊁II
5 6 7 8

⊁III
5 6 7 8

Moving left to right, count the giraffes. Circle the fourth giraffe. Draw a line under the eighth giraffe.

Larger or Smaller
Color the chick with the smaller number yellow.

SKIP-COUNT BY
2's.

SAY THE NUMBERS OUT LOUD.

2
4
6
8
10
12
14
16
18
20

COLOR NUMBERS 7 AND 8

 1 2 3 4 5 6 7 8 9

Numbers

The **+** sign means you should add. Look at each of the groups below and count the number of animals in each one. Write the correct number on the lines provided and then add the two numbers together to get the sum, or the total.

_____ + _____ = _____

_____ + _____ = _____

_____ + _____ = _____

. . . .

Greater Than or Less Than

Alligators are hungry animals. They always want to eat the bigger number. Think of the open end of the symbol < as the open mouth of an alligator trying to eat the bigger number.

1 **<** 3   4 **>** 2

Now you try. Have the alligator eat the bigger number. Draw a < if the number on the right is bigger or a > if the number on the left is bigger. The first one has been done for you.

4 **>** 1   2 ◯ 3   5 ◯ 4   2 ◯ 4

10 11 12 13 14 15 16 17 18 19 20

9 Nine

Trace the number 9 and the word nine.

9 9 9 nine nine

How many ones do you count?

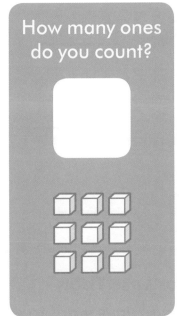

Count the butterflies and color the butterfly labeled number 9.

Circle all the number 9's.

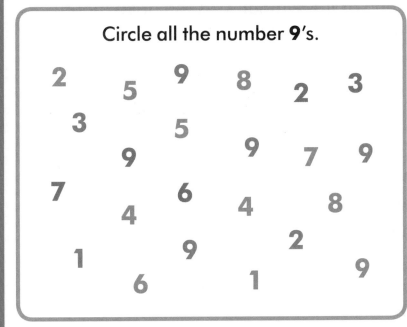

2 5 9 8 2 3
3 5 9 7 9
9 7 9
7 6 4 8
4 2
1 9 9
6 1

9

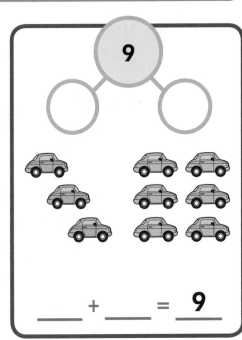

___ + ___ = **9**

NUMBERS & COUNTING

10 Ten

Trace the number **10** and the word **ten**.

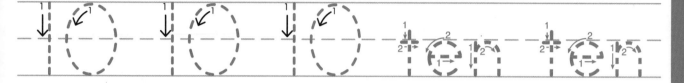

How many **tens** do you count?

How many **ones** do you count?

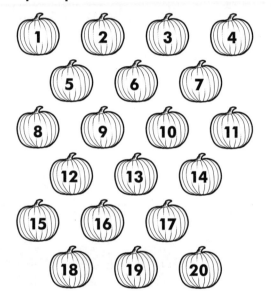

Count the pumpkins and color the pumpkin labeled number **10**.

1 2 3 4
5 6 7
8 9 10 11
12 13 14
15 16 17
18 19 20

Circle all the number **10's**.

10 15 6 10 18
8
4 16 2
20 10 10
6
7 2 9
1 8 10 13

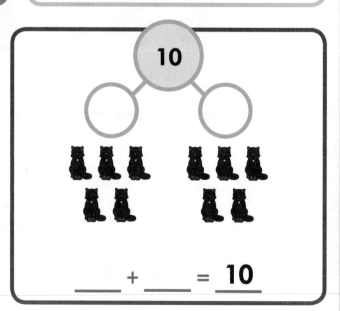

10

_____ + _____ = **10**

195

Numbers

Tally marks are used to count or keep score. They are grouped in sets of five, which makes counting faster. Each | mark equals 1. After there are four | marks, a / mark crosses through them, which equals five.

1	I	6	ⵑ I
2	II	7	ⵑ II
3	III	8	ⵑ III
4	IIII	9	ⵑ IIII
5	ⵑ	10	ⵑ ⵑ

Count the tally marks and circle the correct number.

ⵑ IIII   ⵑ ⵑ

8   9   10   11   8   9   10   11

SKIP-COUNT BY
2's.

SAY THE NUMBERS
OUT LOUD.

Moving left to right, count the apples.
Circle the ninth apple. Draw a line under the tenth apple.

Write these numbers in order. Start with the smallest number.

5   9   3   4

2   10   6   7

COLOR
NUMBERS
9 AND 10

 1 2 3 4 5 6 7 8 9

Numbers

Count the bugs below. Write the number of bugs in each row in the box at right.

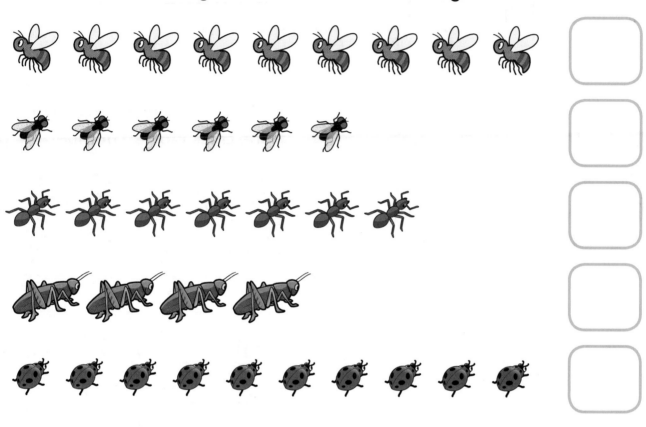

Fill in the missing numbers below.

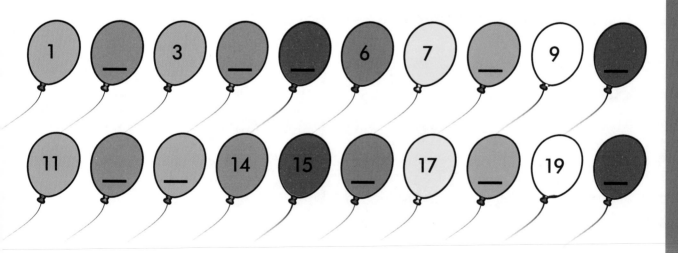

10 11 12 13 14 15 16 17 18 19 20

11 Eleven

Trace the number **11** and the word **eleven**.

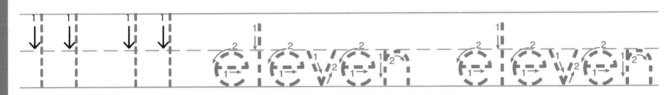

How many **tens** do you count?

How many **ones** do you count?

Count the chicks and color the chick labeled number **11**.

1 2 3 4
5 6 7 8
9 10 11 12
13 14 15 16
17 18 19 20

Circle all the number **11**'s.

20 3 10 11
11 8
7 10 18 11
9 2 1
11 6 6
6 16 11 13

11

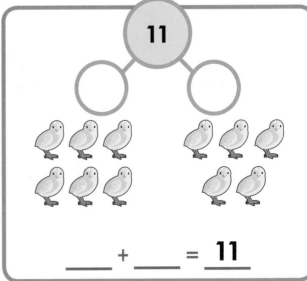

___ + ___ = **11**

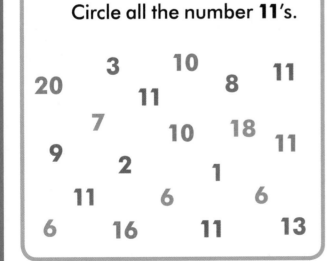

1 2 3 4 5 6 7 8 9

12 Twelve

Trace the number **12** and the word **twelve**.

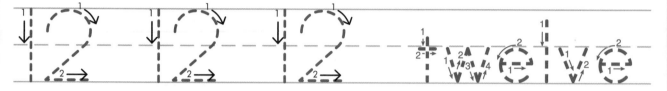

How many **tens** do you count?

How many **ones** do you count?

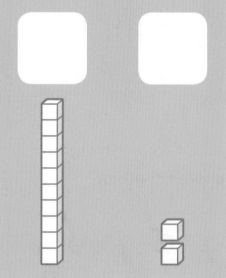

Count the chickens and color the chicken labeled number **12**.

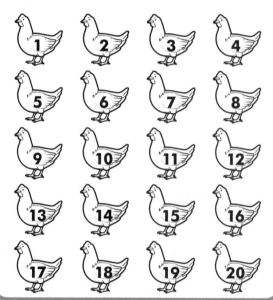

1 2 3 4
5 6 7 8
9 10 11 12
13 14 15 16
17 18 19 20

Circle all the number **12**'s.

12   1   6   4
      13   12
   8   9
10   12   7
   3   20
17   16   2
5   12   11   12

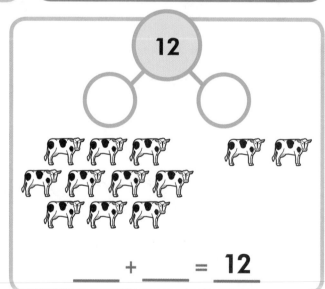

12

_____ + _____ = **12**

10 11 12 13 14 15 16 17 18 19 20

Numbers

Tally marks are used to count or keep score. They are grouped in sets of five, which makes counting faster. Each | mark equals 1. After there are four | marks, a / mark crosses through them, which equals five.

1	I	6	ⵀ I
2	II	7	ⵀ II
3	III	8	ⵀ III
4	IIII	9	ⵀ IIII
5	ⵀ	10	ⵀ ⵀ

Count the tally marks and circle the correct number.

ⵀ ⵀ I

9   10   11   12

ⵀ ⵀ II

9   10   11   12

SKIP-COUNT BY
2's.

SAY THE NUMBERS
OUT LOUD.

Moving left to right, count the guitars. Circle the eighth guitar. Draw a line under the twelfth guitar.

Count the pencils. Color a square for each pencil on the graph below.

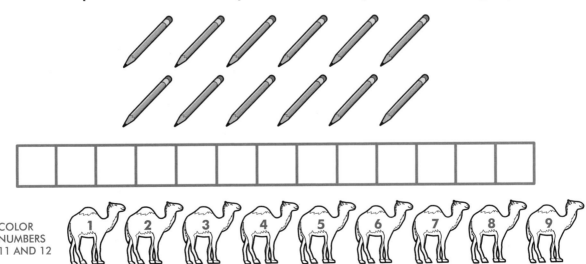

COLOR
NUMBERS
11 AND 12

Numbers

Count the shells on the beach. Fill in the boxes
of the graph to show the number of shells.

Circle which shell
appears on the
beach more.

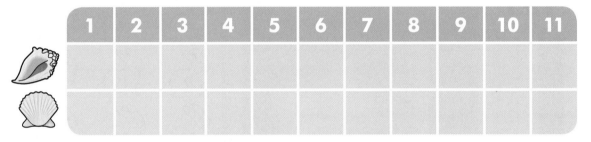

	1	2	3	4	5	6	7	8	9	10	11

Write these numbers in order from smallest to largest.

3   6   4   9

9   2   5   1

8   7   10   2

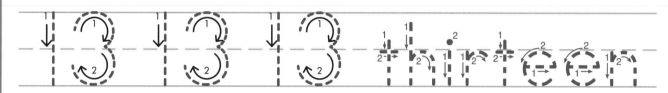 **13** **Thirteen**

Trace the number **13** and the word **thirteen**.

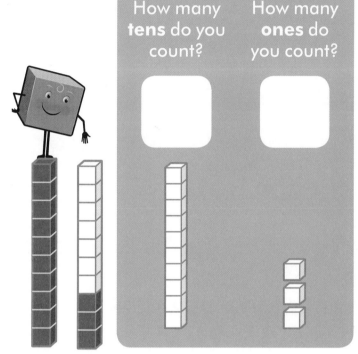

How many **tens** do you count?

How many **ones** do you count?

Count the rabbits and color the rabbit labeled number 13.

Circle all the number **13**'s.

13   7   10   2
    12   4
  1   15
      13   18
8   17   6
  5   9   13
14   13   16   20

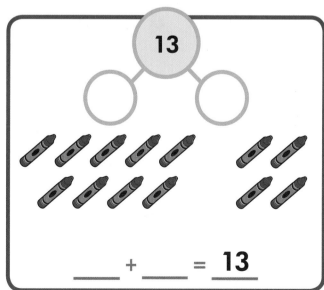

13

_____ + _____ = **13**

   4

14 Fourteen

Trace the number **14** and the word **fourteen**.

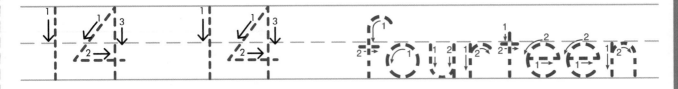

How many **tens** do you count?

How many **ones** do you count?

Count the deer and color the deer labeled number **14**.

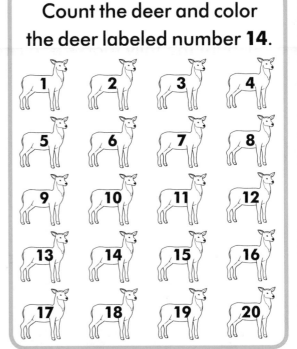

Circle all the number **14**'s.

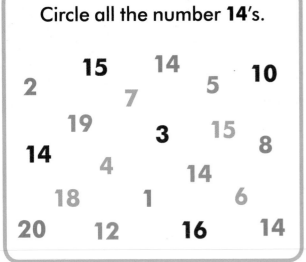

15   14   10
2   7   5
19   3   15   8
14   4   14
18   1   6
20   12   16   14

14

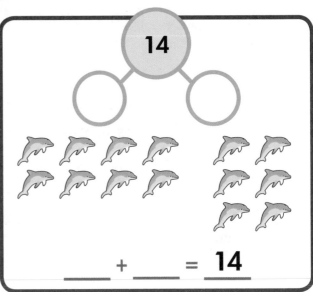

_____ + _____ = **14**

10 11 12 13 14 15 16 17 18 19 20

203

Numbers

Tally marks are used to count or keep score. They are grouped in sets of five, which makes counting faster. Each | mark equals 1. After there are four | marks, a / mark crosses through them, which equals five.

1	I	6	⊣⊦⊦ I
2	II	7	⊣⊦⊦ II
3	III	8	⊣⊦⊦ III
4	IIII	9	⊣⊦⊦ IIII
5	⊣⊦⊦	10	⊣⊦⊦ ⊣⊦⊦

Count the tally marks and circle the correct number.

⊣⊦⊦ ⊣⊦⊦ III   ⊣⊦⊦ ⊣⊦⊦ IIII

9   10   11   9   10   11
12   13   14   12   13   14

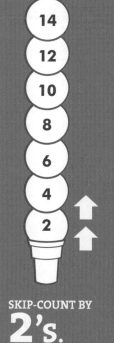

Moving left to right and top to bottom, count the hearts.
Circle the eleventh heart.
Draw a line under the fourteenth heart.

SKIP-COUNT BY
2's.

SAY THE NUMBERS
OUT LOUD.

Read the clues below. Draw a line from
the clue to the correct answer.

7

The number is one greater than 2.

5

The number is one less than 9.

3

8

The number is one less than 6.

Numbers

Color the snowman with the **smallest number**.

Write the **smallest number**.

_____

- -

_____

Write the **largest number**.

_____

- -

_____

Fill in the missing numbers on the number lines below.

9 _____ 11 _____

10 11 12 13 14 15 16 17 18 19 20

15 Fifteen

Trace the number **15** and the word **fifteen**.

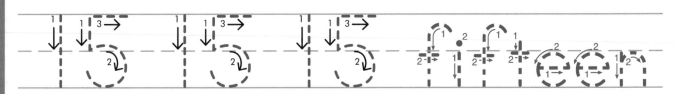

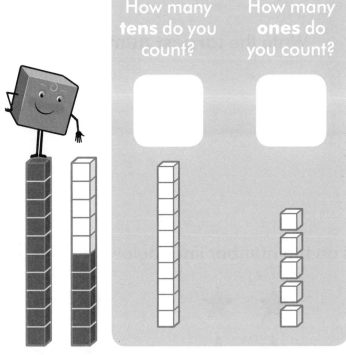

How many **tens** do you count?

How many **ones** do you count?

Count the acorns and color the acorn labeled number **15**.

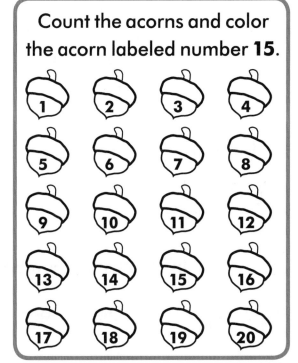

Circle all the number **15**'s.

7   11
2   15
5   12
1
4   20
10   6
17
15
10   8   18
15   12   18   3

15

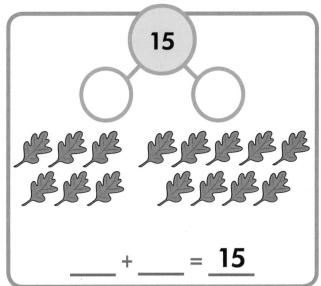

____ + ____ = **15**

16 Sixteen

Trace the number **16** and the word **sixteen**.

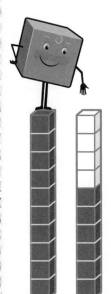

How many **tens** do you count?

How many **ones** do you count?

Count the dogs and color the dog labeled number **16**.

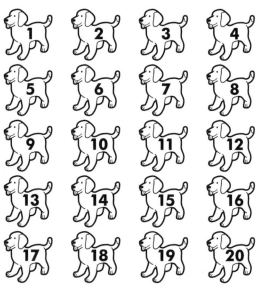

Circle all the number **16**'s.

16   1   **10**   15   16
   5
11   14   **12**   16
7   **18**   16
9   20   13
6   16   2   6

16

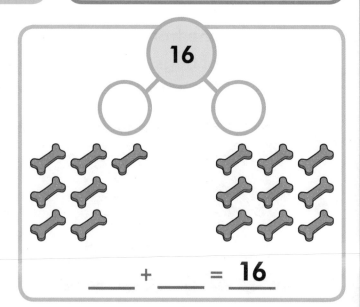

_____ + _____ = **16**

Numbers

Tally marks are used to count or keep score. They are grouped in sets of five, which makes counting faster. Each | mark equals 1. After there are four | marks, a / mark crosses through them, which equals five.

1	I	6	̶I̶I̶I̶I̶ I
2	II	7	̶I̶I̶I̶I̶ II
3	III	8	̶I̶I̶I̶I̶ III
4	IIII	9	̶I̶I̶I̶I̶ IIII
5	̶I̶I̶I̶I̶	10	̶I̶I̶I̶I̶ ̶I̶I̶I̶I̶

Count the tally marks and circle the correct number.

̶I̶I̶I̶I̶ ̶I̶I̶I̶I̶ ̶I̶I̶I̶I̶   ̶I̶I̶I̶I̶ ̶I̶I̶I̶I̶ ̶I̶I̶I̶I̶ I

10 11 12 13   10 11 12 13
14 15 16 17 18   14 15 16 17 18

Moving left to right and top to bottom, count the hot dogs. Circle the tenth hot dog. Draw a line under the sixteenth hot dog.

Draw a line from each number to the matching number of bugs. Then draw a line from the bugs to the correct number of tally marks.

13 ̶I̶I̶I̶I̶ ̶I̶I̶I̶I̶ ̶I̶I̶I̶I̶ I

16 ̶I̶I̶I̶I̶ ̶I̶I̶I̶I̶ ̶I̶I̶I̶I̶

15 ̶I̶I̶I̶I̶ ̶I̶I̶I̶I̶ III

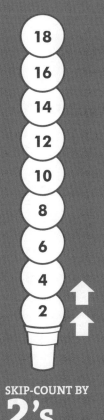

18
16
14
12
10
8
6
4
2

SKIP-COUNT BY
2's.

SAY THE NUMBERS
OUT LOUD.

Numbers

_____ How many 13's do you see?

_____ How many 14's do you see?

_____ How many 15's do you see?

_____ How many 16's do you see?

16	13	15	6	7
5	16	14	9	15
15	13	8	13	15

Larger or Smaller

Color the lily pad with the smaller number **green**.

 14

 15

The **+** sign means you should add. Look at each of the groups below and count the number of animals. Write the correct number on the lines provided and then add the two numbers together to get the sum, or the total.

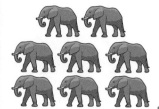 _____ + _____ = _____

_____ + _____ = _____

10 11 12 13 14 15 16 17 18 19 20

17 Seventeen

Trace the number **17** and the word **seventeen**.

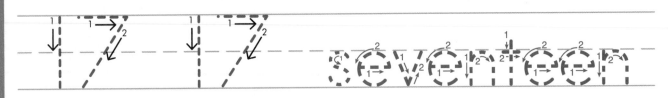

How many **tens** do you count?

How many **ones** do you count?

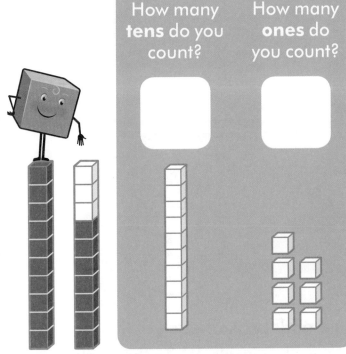

Count the drums and color the drum labeled number **17**.

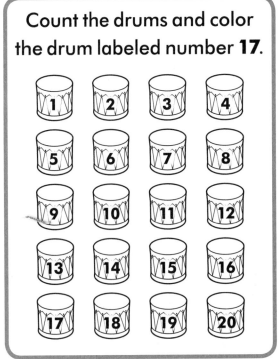

Circle all the number **17**'s.

2	10	9 17
	15	7
17	1	11 16
2	18	20
9	14	6
13	17	4

17

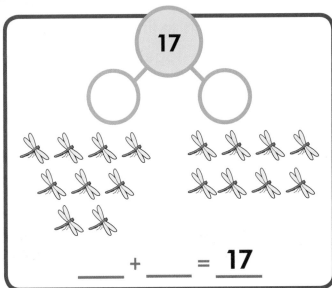

_____ + _____ = **17**

18 Eighteen

Trace the number **18** and the word **eighteen**.

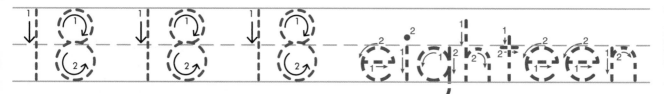

How many **tens** do you count?

How many **ones** do you count?

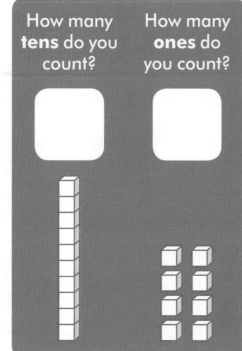

Count the ducks and color the duck labeled number **18**.

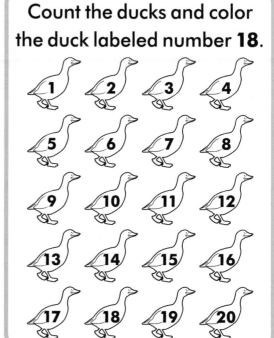

1 2 3 4
5 6 7 8
9 10 11 12
13 14 15 16
17 18 19 20

Circle all the number **18**'s.

1
18   12   10
15   4
15   20   14
11   18
18   17
6   4   16
4   13   13   2

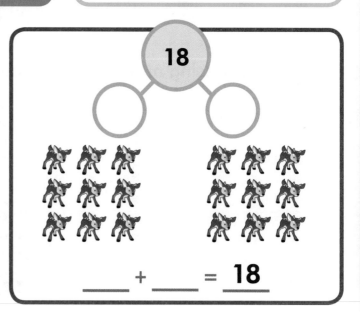

18

_____ + _____ = **18**

Numbers

Tally marks are used to count or keep score. They are grouped in sets of five, which makes counting faster. Each | mark equals 1. After there are four | marks, a / mark crosses through them, which equals five.

1	I	6	ꗲ I
2	II	7	ꗲ II
3	III	8	ꗲ III
4	IIII	9	ꗲ IIII
5	ꗲ	10	ꗲ ꗲ

Count the tally marks and circle the correct number.

ꗲ ꗲ ꗲ II   ꗲ ꗲ ꗲ III

11 12 13 14 15   11 12 13 14 15
    16 17 18   16 17 18

Moving left to right, count the ice-cream cones.
Circle the fourth ice-cream cone.
Draw a line under the seventeenth ice-cream cone.

Fill in the missing numbers on the number lines below.

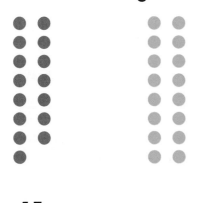

15   **____**   **17**   **____**

20
18
16
14
12
10
8
6
4
2

SKIP-COUNT BY
2's.

SAY THE NUMBERS
OUT LOUD.

COLOR
NUMBERS
17 AND 18

 1   2   3   4   5   6   7   8   9

Numbers

Count the number of sea creatures, then
color the correct number at right.

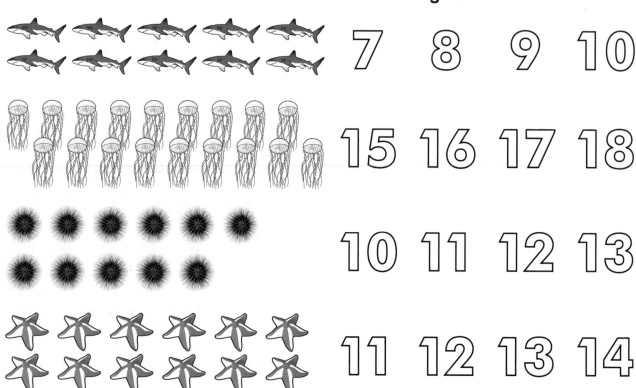

7 8 9 10

15 16 17 18

10 11 12 13

11 12 13 14

Write these numbers in order, from smallest to largest.

6 10 2 12

16 18 5 14

7 13 9 1

10 11 12 13 14 15 16 17 18 19 20

19 Nineteen

Trace the number **19** and the word **nineteen**.

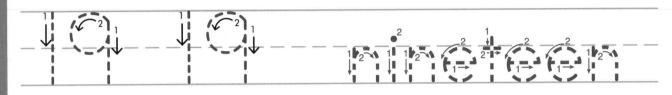

How many **tens** do you count?

How many **ones** do you count?

Count the firefighters' hats and color the hat labeled number **19**.

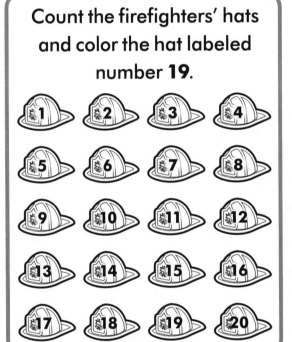

Circle all the number **19**'s.

3 19 6
14 10 2
17 1 16 13
11 20
5 18 19 12
19 15 4

19

____ + ____ = **19**

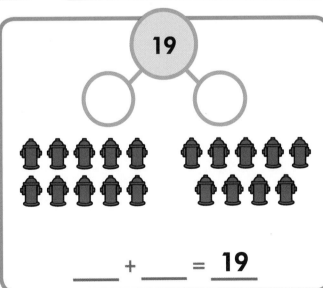

Trace the number **20** and the word **twenty**.

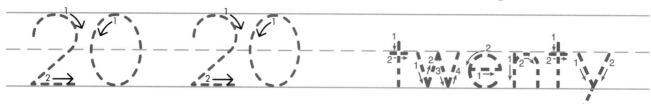

How many **tens** do you count?

How many **ones** do you count?

Count the fishbowls and color the fishbowl labeled number **20**.

1	2	3	4
5	6	7	8
9	10	11	12
13	14	15	16
17	18	19	20

Circle all the number **20**'s.

10   **3**
6   **12**   **9**
    20
15
        5   1
20   **14**
    2
            16
13   **8**   **20**
4   18   11   **19**

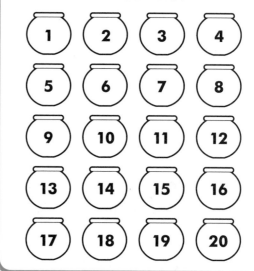

20

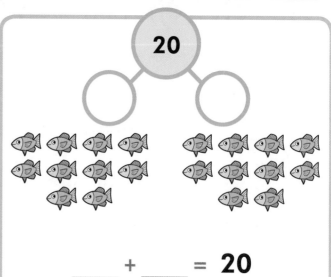

____ + ____ = **20**

10 11 12 13 14 15 16 17 18 19 20

Numbers

Tally marks are used to count or keep score. They are grouped in sets of five, which makes counting faster. Each | mark equals 1. After there are four | marks, a / mark crosses through them, which equals five.

1	I	6	ⅢⅢ I
2	II	7	ⅢⅢ II
3	III	8	ⅢⅢ III
4	IIII	9	ⅢⅢ IIII
5	ⅢⅢ	10	ⅢⅢ ⅢⅢ

Count the tally marks and circle the correct number.

ⅢⅢ ⅢⅢ ⅢⅢ IIII   ⅢⅢ ⅢⅢ ⅢⅢ ⅢⅢ

16   17   18   19   20   16   17   18   19   20

· ·

Moving left to right and top to bottom, count the spiders.
Circle the first spider. Draw a line under the twentieth spider.

· ·

Read the clues below. Draw a line from the clue to the correct answer.

17   **This number is one greater than 18.**   **18**

This number is one less than 19.

19   **This number is one greater than 16.**   **20**

COLOR
NUMBERS
19 AND 20

Numbers

Help the bird get to her egg by following the numbers from **1** to **20** in order.

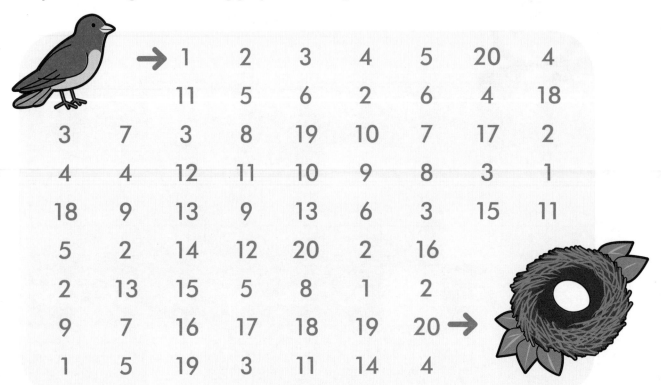

		1	2	3	4	5	20	4
		11	5	6	2	6	4	18
3	7	3	8	19	10	7	17	2
4	4	12	11	10	9	8	3	1
18	9	13	9	13	6	3	15	11
5	2	14	12	20	2	16		
2	13	15	5	8	1	2		
9	7	16	17	18	19	20		
1	5	19	3	11	14	4		

Skip-count by **2**'s, **3**'s, and **5**'s.

2's
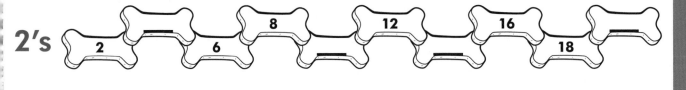
2, 6, 8, ___, 12, ___, 16, 18, ___

3's

___, 6, ___, 12, ___, ___

5's

___, 10, ___, 20

| 10 | 11 | 12 | 13 | 14 | 15 | 16 | 17 | 18 | 19 | 20 |

217

Let's Count to 100!

Count up to 100, filling in the numbers that are missing.

1	2	3	4	5	6	7		9	10
11	12	13	14		16	17	18	19	20
21	22		24	25	26	27	28	29	30
31	32	33		35	36	37	38	39	40
41	42	43	44	45	46	47		49	50
51	52	53		55	56	57	58	59	60
61		63	64	65	66	67	68	69	70
71	72	73	74	75		77	78	79	80
81	82		84	85	86	87	88	89	90
91	92	93	94	95	96	97	98		100

COLORS & SHAPES

Colors

Primary Colors
There are three primary colors: **red**, **blue**, and yellow.
Primary colors cannot be created from any other colors.

red   blue   yellow

Secondary Colors
When you mix two primary colors, you can make secondary colors! Mix the colors to guess what color you get. Trace the color words below.

 = orange

 = green

 = purple

Yellow

Trace the word yellow.

Color in the objects that are yellow.

I see a yellow…

Count how many items are yellow and record them on your ten frame.

Amazing Color Sentences

Trace the sentence. Color the fish .

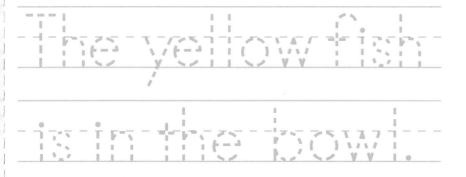

The yellow fish is in the bowl.

Now write a sentence of your own.

Circle

A **circle** is round.
Practice drawing circles by tracing the circles below.

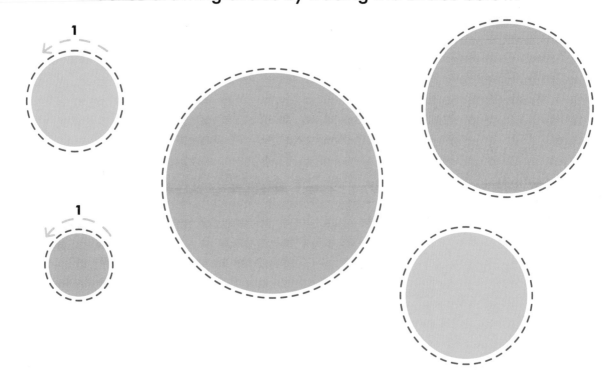

Trace the word **circle**.

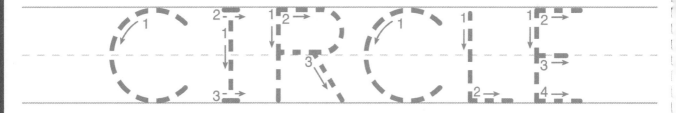

Color the circles below yellow.

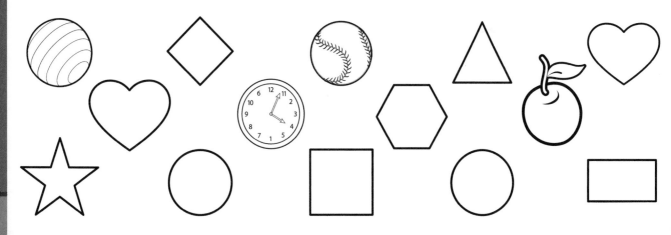

Blue

Trace the word **blue**.

Count how many balloons are **blue** and record them on your ten frame.

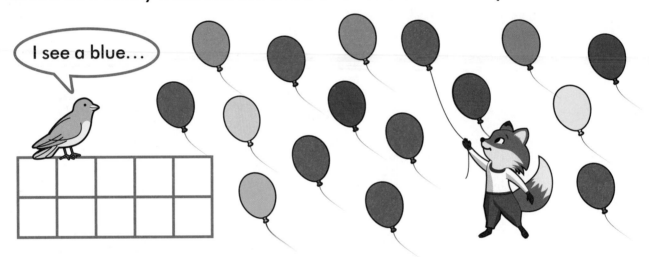

I see a blue…

Amazing Color Sentences

Trace the sentence. Color the bird .

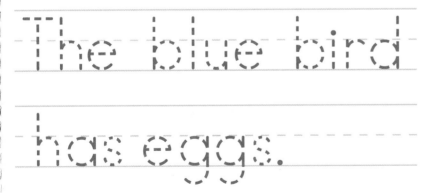

Now write a sentence of your own.

Square

A **square** has four sides of equal length.
Practice drawing **squares** by tracing the dotted lines below.

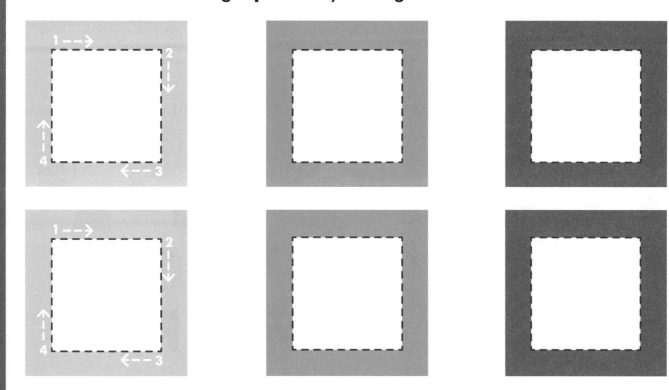

Trace the word **square**.

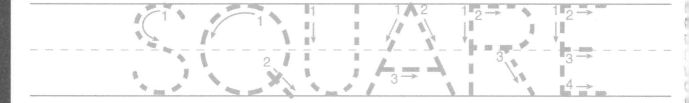

Trace the **squares** and color them **blue**.

Red

Trace the word **red**.

Color in the things that are **red**.

I see a red…

Count how many items are **red** and record them on your ten frame.

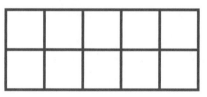

Amazing Color Sentences

Trace the sentence. Color the tomatoes .

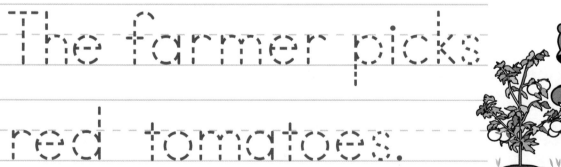

The farmer picks red tomatoes.

Now write a sentence of your own.

225

Heart

Practice drawing **hearts** by tracing the dotted lines below.

Trace the word **heart**.

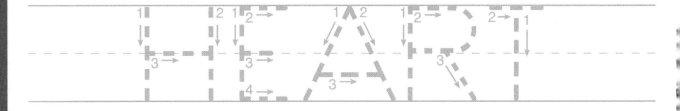

Trace the **hearts** below and then decorate the last cookie yourself.

Green

Trace the word **green**.

green   green

Color in the things that are **green**.

I see a green…

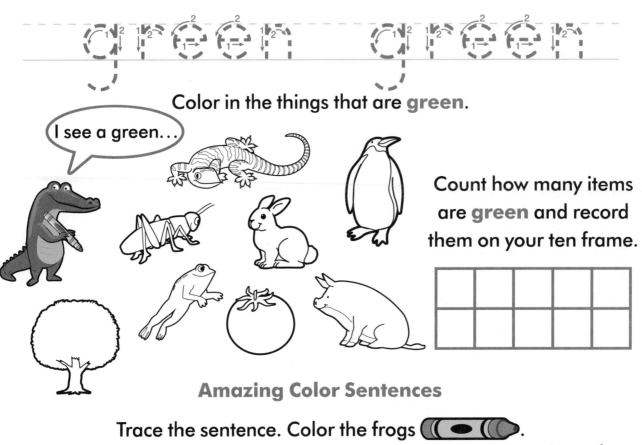

Count how many items are **green** and record them on your ten frame.

Amazing Color Sentences

Trace the sentence. Color the frogs.

The green frog hops.

Now write a sentence of your own.

Rectangle

A **rectangle** has four sides. Two sides are long. Two sides are short. Practice drawing **rectangles** by tracing the dotted lines below.

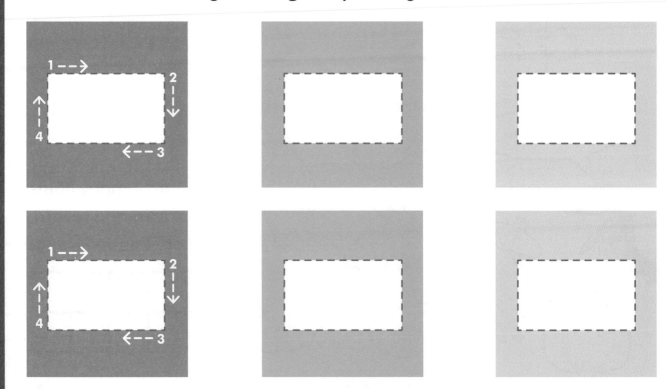

Trace the word **rectangle**.

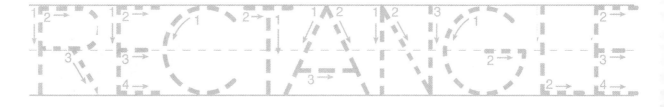

Trace the **rectangle**. Now color the train car.

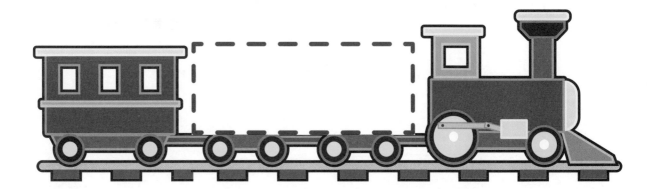

Black

Trace the word **black**.

Color in the things that are **black**.

I see a black...

Count how many items are **black** and record them on your ten frame.

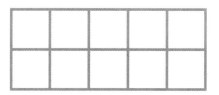

Amazing Color Sentences

Trace the sentence. Color the spider .

Now write a sentence of your own.

Oval

Practice drawing **ovals** by tracing the **ovals** below.

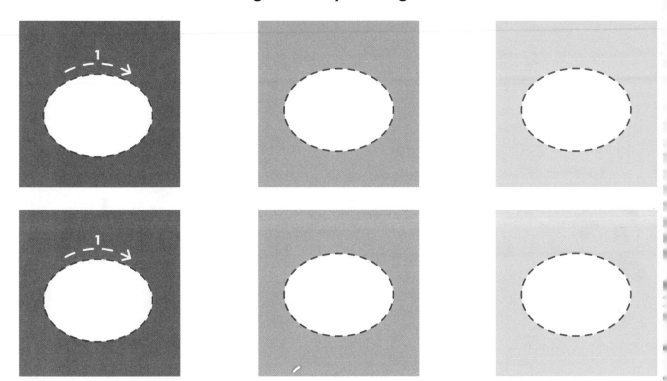

Trace the word **oval**.

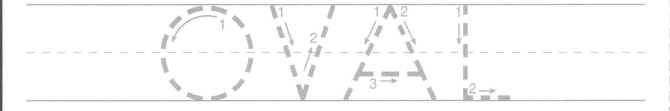

The spider has an **oval** body. Trace the oval and color it **black**.

COLORS & SHAPES

230

Orange

Trace the word orange.

Count how many cars are orange and record them on your ten frame.

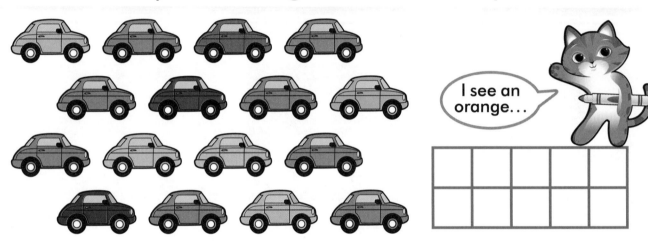

I see an orange...

Amazing Color Sentences

Trace the sentence. Color the jack-o'-lantern .

The orange

jack-o-lantern is lit up.

Now write a sentence of your own.

Star

Trace the **stars**.

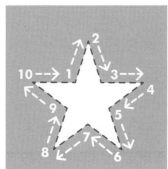

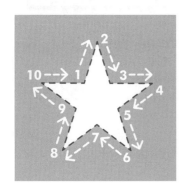

Trace the word **star**.

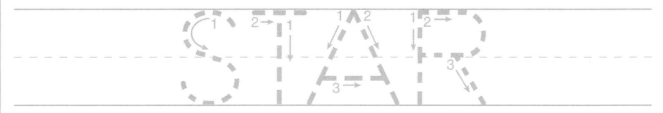

Color in the last **star** to complete the pattern.

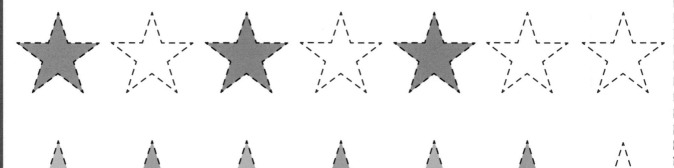

Purple

Trace the word **purple**.

purple   purple

Color in the things that are **purple**.

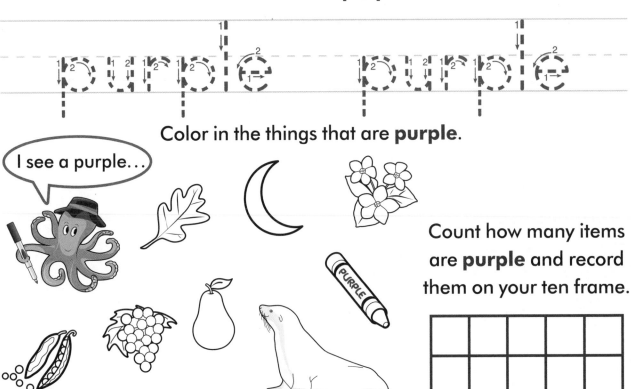

I see a purple…

Count how many items are **purple** and record them on your ten frame.

Amazing Color Sentences

Trace the sentence. Color the flowers .

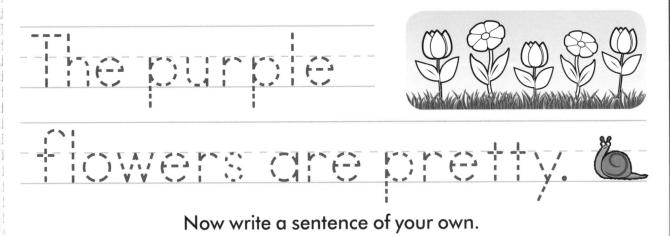

The purple flowers are pretty.

Now write a sentence of your own.

Triangle

A **triangle** has three sides.
Practice drawing **triangles** by tracing the **triangles** below.

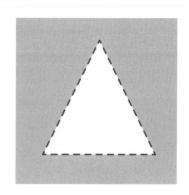
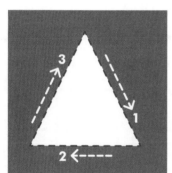

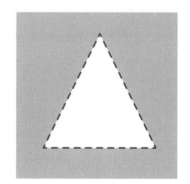

Trace the word **triangle**.

Color the seven **triangles** below **purple**.

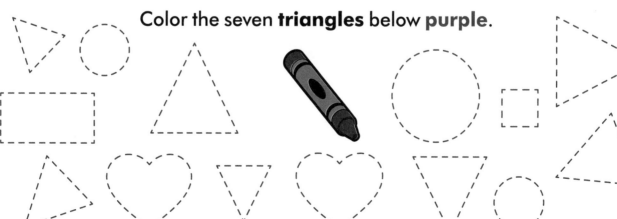

Pink

Trace the word **pink**.

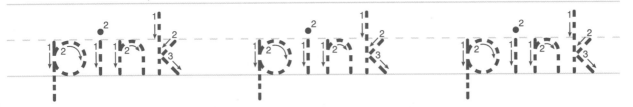

Count how many hearts are **pink** and record them on your ten frame.

I see a pink...

Amazing Color Sentences

Trace the sentence. Color the birthday cake .

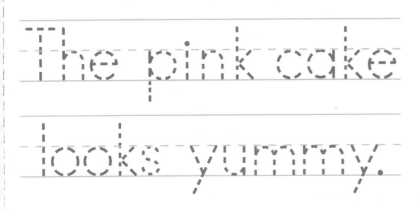

The pink cake looks yummy.

Now write a sentence of your own.

235

You Can Color

Let's get ready to paint. First, we need to add all the **colors** to the palette. Color them.

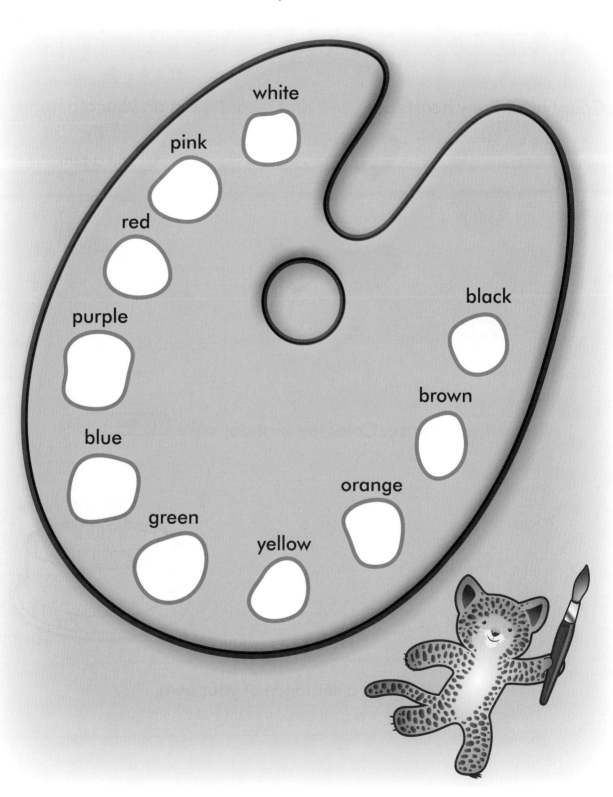

white

pink

red

purple

blue

green

yellow

orange

black

brown

Missing Colors

What colors are missing from the rainbow?
Color them.

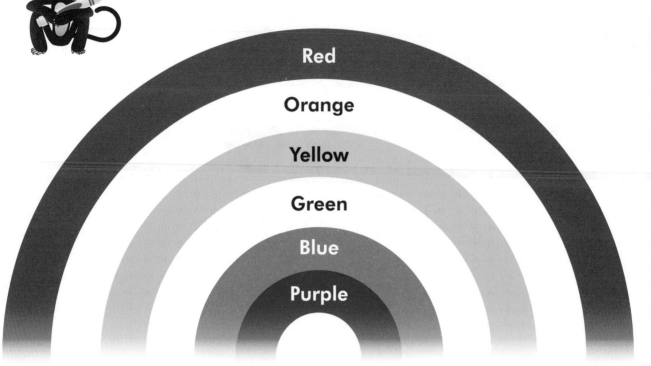

Red

Orange

Yellow

Green

Blue

Purple

Trace the color words below.

Colors and Shapes

I Know My Colors and Shapes

Trace the shape words.

Square   Circle

Triangle   Heart

 Color the squares **green**. How many are there? _____

 Color the triangles **yellow**. How many are there? _____

 Color the circles **blue**. How many are there? _____

 Color the hearts **red**. How many are there? _____

Colors and Shapes

I Know My Colors and Shapes

Trace the shape words.

Rectangle   Oval

Diamond   Heart

 Color the rectangles **purple**. How many are there? _____

 Color the ovals **orange**. How many are there? _____

 Color the diamonds **black**. How many are there? _____

 Color the hearts **pink**. How many are there? _____

Finish the Shapes

Finish the shape and color it.	Now you draw the shape.	Trace the word.
		Rectangle
		Square
		Triangle
		Circle
		Heart
		Diamond

2-D Shapes

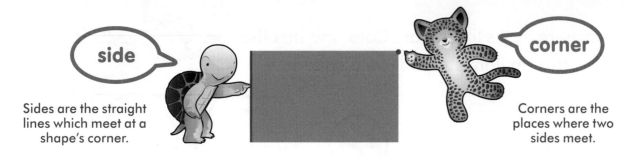

side

Sides are the straight lines which meet at a shape's corner.

corner

Corners are the places where two sides meet.

Color each shape. Then write the correct number of sides and corners for each shape.

Sides _____

Corners _____

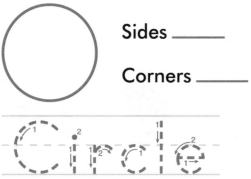

Sides _____

Corners _____

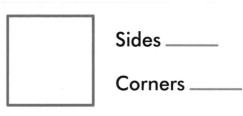

Sides _____

Corners _____

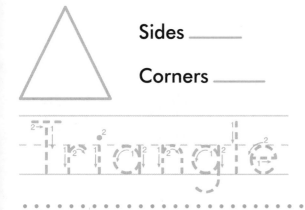

Sides _____

Corners _____

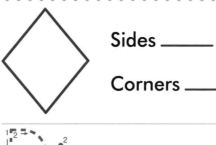

Sides _____

Corners _____

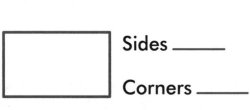

Sides _____

Corners _____

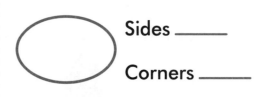

3-D Shapes

A sphere looks like a ball. Color the box that has an item shaped like a sphere.

A cube looks like a wooden block. Color the box that has an item shaped like a cube.

A cylinder looks like a can of soda. Color the box that has an item shaped like a cylinder.

A cone looks like a bottom of an ice-cream cone. Color the box that has an item shaped like a cone.

3-D Shapes

Trace the 3-D shapes below. Then color the shapes the correct color using the key.

 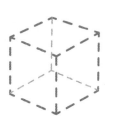  

cone   sphere   cube   cylinder

How many shapes did you color?

cone _____   sphere _____   cube _____   cylinder _____

243

3-D Shapes

Look at each shape and then write the correct number of faces, vertices, and edges for each shape. The first one has been done for you,

face

Faces are the shape's surfaces.

edge

Edges are the line segments where two faces meet.

vertice

Vertices are the places where three or more edges meet.

faces __6__

edges __12__

vertices __8__

Cube

faces _____

edges _____

vertices _____

Sphere

faces _____

edges _____

vertices _____

Cone

faces _____

edges _____

vertices _____

Rectangular

Prism

TIME & DATE

Telling Time

A clock shows twelve hours, which is half a day.
Fill in the missing hours.

Telling Time

minute hand (long) · · · · · · · · · · · · · ·   · · · · · · · · · · · · · · hour hand (short)

Look at the hands on each clock.
Then color in the box with the correct time.

3:00
5:00

5:00
6:00

9:00
11:00

12:00
2:00

1:00
3:00

10:00
9:00

Telling Time

minute hand
(long)

hour hand
(short)

Look at the hands on each clock.
Then color in the box with the correct time.

2:00

5:00

12:00

8:00

7:00

4:00

6:00

8:00

10:00

5:00

11:00

7:00

What Time Is It?

Look at each of the clocks below. Write the correct time on the line provided. Remember, the short hand is the hour hand. The first one has been done for you.

7 :00   ___ :00   ___ :00

___ :00   ___ :00   ___ :00

___ :00   ___ :00   ___ :00

School Time
Draw the hands on the clock to show what time school begins.

249

What Time Is It?

Look at each of the times below. Draw the hour hands on the clocks to show the correct time. The first one has been done for you.

4:00

8:00

5:00

9:00

11:00

6:00

2:00

12:00

1:00

Sleep Time
Draw the hands on the clock to show your bedtime.

What Time Is It?

Look at the hands on each clock. Then draw a line to the box with its matching time. Remember, the small hand is the hour hand.

1:00
3:00
12:00

5:00
6:00
8:00

6:00
9:00
12:00

8:00
10:00
2:00

1:00
3:00
5:00

2:00
10:00
9:00

251

What Time Is It?

Look at the hands on each clock.
Then draw a line to the digital clock with its matching time.

What Time Is It?

Look at each of the clocks below. Write the correct time on the line provided. Remember, the small hand is the hour hand. The first one has been done for you.

8 :00

_____ :00

_____ :00

_____ :00

_____ :00

_____ :00

_____ :00

_____ :00

_____ :00

Lunchtime
Draw the hands on the
clock to show what time
you eat lunch.

What Time Is It?

Look at each of the times below. Draw the hour hands on the clocks to show the correct time. The first one has been done for you.

5:00

7:00

3:00

10:00

12:00

6:00

1:00

11:00

4:00

Playtime
Draw the hands on the clock to show a time when you play.

Days of the Week

Practice writing the days of the week.

Sunday **Monday** **Tuesday** **Wednesday**

Thursday **Friday** **Saturday**

Circle what day it will be tomorrow.

Sunday **Monday** **Tuesday** **Wednesday**

Thursday **Friday** **Saturday**

Days of the Week

Find the names of the days of the week in the word search puzzle below. The words go across, down, and diagonally.

Sunday   **Monday**   **Tuesday**   **Wednesday**
Thursday   **Friday**   **Saturday**

```
Y  L  M  O  N  D  A  Y  W  X
W  E  D  N  E  S  D  A  Y  V
N  P  M  A  X  M  Y  P  G  S
E  F  A  P  R  A  L  E  H  U
T  U  E  S  D  A  Y  K  C  N
B  U  C  I  F  I  V  M  E  D
E  T  R  A  G  W  E  N  M  A
J  F  S  A  T  U  R  D  A  Y
T  H  U  R  S  D  A  Y  E  E
```

Circle what day it is today.

Sunday   **Monday**   **Tuesday**

Wednesday   **Thursday**   **Friday**

Saturday

Days of the Week

Solve the riddle below by filling in the correct letter for each number.

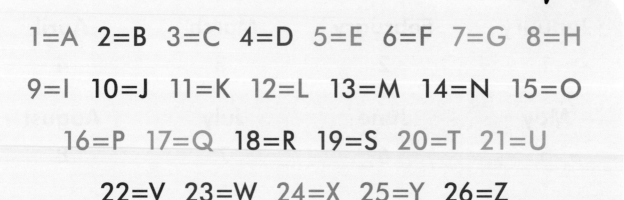

1=A 2=B 3=C 4=D 5=E 6=F 7=G 8=H

9=I 10=J 11=K 12=L 13=M 14=N 15=O

16=P 17=Q 18=R 19=S 20=T 21=U

22=V 23=W 24=X 25=Y 26=Z

Name three days in a row without using the words Monday, Tuesday, Wednesday, Thursday, Friday, Saturday, or Sunday.

___ ___ ___ ___ ___ ___ ___ ___ ___ ,
25   5   19 20   5   18   4   1   25

___ ___ ___ ___ ___ , and
20 15   4   1   25

___ ___ ___ ___ ___ ___ ___ ___ ___ !
20 15 13 15 18 18 15 23

Circle what day it was yesterday.

Sunday   **Monday**   **Tuesday**   **Wednesday**

Thursday   **Friday**   **Saturday**

Months of the Year

There are twelve months in a year. Months are proper nouns and need to be **capitalized**.

January 1	**February** 2	**March** 3	**April** 4
May 5	**June** 6	**July** 7	**August** 8
September 9	**October** 10	**November** 11	**December** 12

What is the first month of the year?

_____

In what month is your birthday?

_____

In what month is the last day of school?

_____

What is the last month of the year?

_____

What month comes after April?

_____

Months of the Year

Look at the names of the months
and trace them in order.

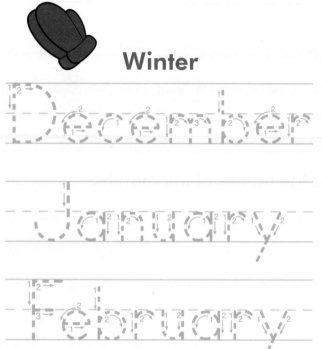

Winter

December

January

February

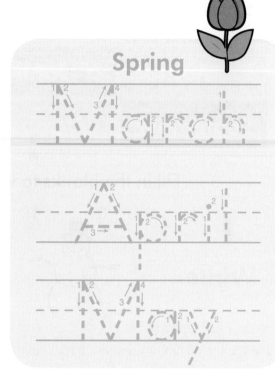

Spring

March

April

May

Summer

June

July

August

Fall

September

October

November

Months of the Year

The four seasons are: **Winter Spring Summer Fall**

January	February	March	April
May	June	July	August
September	October	November	December

Fill in the blanks to write the names of the months.

Winter

D __ __ e m __ __ __

J __ __ __ __ __ __ __

__ e b __ __ __ __ __ __

Spring

M __ __ __ __ __

A __ __ __ __ __

__ a y

Summer

J __ __ e

__ u l __

A __ __ __ __ __ t

Fall

S __ p t __ __ __ __ __

O __ t __ __ __ __

__ __ v e m __ __ __

Fourth of July

The Fourth of July is a day to celebrate America's birthday.
It is the day we gained our independence from Britain.
Circle the symbol of America in each row that is different.

The flag of the United States is a symbol of freedom.
Color in the spaces with the letter **A red** and the
spaces with the letter **B blue** in the American flag below.

Halloween

Halloween is celebrated on October 31.
Color the jack-o'-lantern below.

Use the alphabet code to solve the secret riddle.

A=1 B=2 C=3 D=4 E=5 F=6 G=7 H=8 I=9 J=10

K=11 L=12 M=13 N=14 O=15 P=16 Q=17 R=18

S=19 T=20 U=21 V=22 W=23 X=24 Y=25 Z=26

What was the favorite game at the ghosts' birthday party?

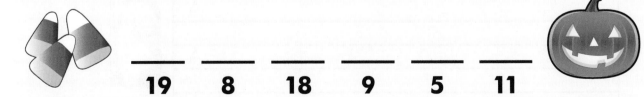

__ __ __ __   __ __ __
8 9 4 5   1 14 4

__ __ __ __ __ __
19 8 18 9 5 11

Thanksgiving

Thanksgiving is a day for giving thanks.
People give thanks for all the good things that they have
received during the year, and celebrate with feasting.

What are YOU thankful for this year?
Have your mom or dad help you write down what
you are thankful for on the lines below.

- -

- -

- -

- -

- -

263

Happy Holidays

People celebrate many different holidays based on their beliefs. What holiday do you celebrate in winter?

Draw a picture of a decoration used during the holiday.

Draw a picture of a special food you eat during the holiday.

Valentine's Day

Valentine's Day is celebrated on February 14. Use the alphabet code to solve the secret message about Valentine's Day.

A=1 B=2 C=3 D=4 E=5 F=6 G=7 H=8

I=9 J=10 K=11 L=12 M=13 N=14 O=15

P=16 Q=17 R=18 S=19 T=20 U=21

V=22 W=23 X=24 Y=25 Z=26

___ ___ ___ ___   ___ ___ ___
23   9   12 12   25 15 21

___ ___   ___ ___
 2   5   13 25

___ ___ ___ ___ ___ ___ ___ ___ ___
22   1 12   5 14 20   9 14   5

?

Decorate the Valentine's Day cookies below.

ME & MY WORLD

All About Me

Draw a picture of yourself using the outline below.
Look in the mirror first. What color eyes and hair do you have?
Is your skin light or dark? Do you have short hair or long?
What makes you **you**?

All About Me

This Is Me

My name is ....

I like to be called ....

My favorite food is ....

My favorite color is ....

My favorite sport is ....

My favorite book is ....

My favorite animal is ....

My favorite game is ....

My best friend's name is ....

All About Me

**Fill in the information below
all about you and where you live.**

My Name . . . .

My Street Address . . . .

. . . .

My City or Town . . . .

My State . . . .

My Country . . . .

I know my phone number!

___ ___ ___ - ___ ___ ___ - ___ ___ ___ ___

Use your fingers to tap your phone number.

When Is Your Birthday?

Circle the month and day of **your birthday**.

January	February	March	April
May	June	July	August
September	October	November	December

1 2 3 4 5 6 7 8

9 10 11 12 13 14 15 16

17 18 19 20 21 22 23 24

25 26 27 28 29 30 31

Draw candles on the top of the cake—one for each year of your age. **Now decorate your cake!**

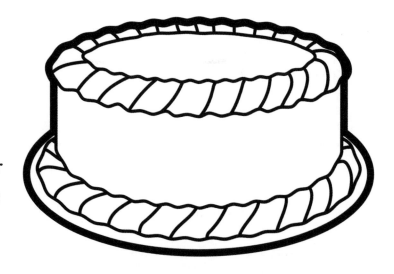

My Birthday

Fill in the blanks below.

On my next birthday I will be turning .... years old.

When I blow out my candles, I will wish for

....

The best  I ever got for my birthday was

....

Find and circle the birthday party words from the word box in the word search below. The words may go across or down.

BALLOONS HAT CAKE CANDLES
ICE CREAM GAMES FRIENDS PRESENTS

W	C	F	I	C	E	C	R	E	A	M	H
B	A	L	L	O	O	N	S	Z	H	X	A
T	K	H	I	C	A	N	D	L	E	S	T
H	E	M	D	A	F	R	I	E	N	D	S
P	R	E	S	E	N	T	S	V	O	T	H
C	E	J	P	M	K	G	A	M	E	S	V

Morning and Night Routine

Look at the pictures below showing the Rascal the Raccoon
getting ready in the morning. Write 1, 2, 3,
and 4 to put them in the right order.

Look at the pictures below showing Zippy the Zebra
getting ready to go to bed. Write 1, 2, 3, and 4
to put them in the right order.

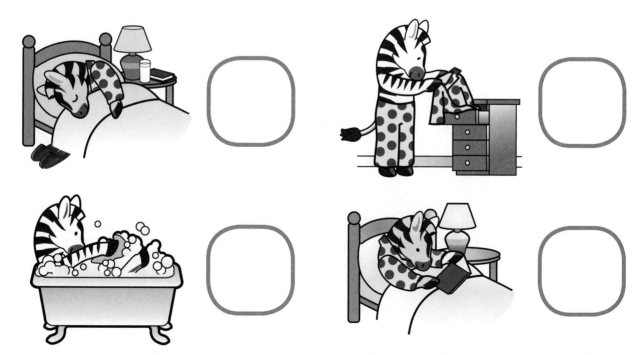

Exercise Is Fun!

Exercise is fun and keeps you healthy!
Exercise helps strengthen your bones and muscles and keeps your heart healthy. There are many ways to exercise that are fun as long as you keep active or moving! Look at the pictures below. Circle **active** or **not active** under each picture.

Active   Not Active

Active   Not Active

Active   Not Active

Active   Not Active

Active   Not Active

Active   Not Active

Active   Not Active

Active   Not Active

Hand Washing

There are germs on your hands. They are so small you can't see them. Germs can make you sick. If you wash your hands, that kills the germs. Color the germs.

Put the following steps for washing hands in the correct order by putting 1 to 5 in the circles.

1 Wet hands   **2** Use soap   **3** Lather, rub, and count to 20

4 Rinse   **5** Dry off hands with a towel

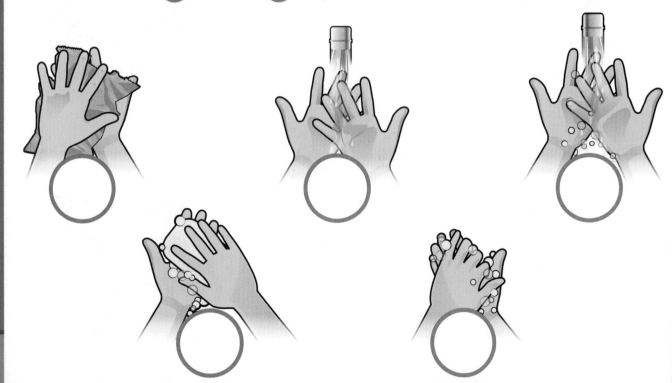

Your Teeth

How many teeth do you have? Count them.

I have _____ upper teeth. I have _____ lower teeth.

I have _____ teeth altogether.

Brush your teeth every morning and night to keep them healthy and clean. Put a number from 1 to 5 in each box to show the correct order in brushing your teeth. Flossing each day also removes food the toothbrush missed.

1 Wet brush   **2** Squeeze toothpaste   **3** Brush teeth

4 Spit toothpaste   **5** Rinse toothbrush

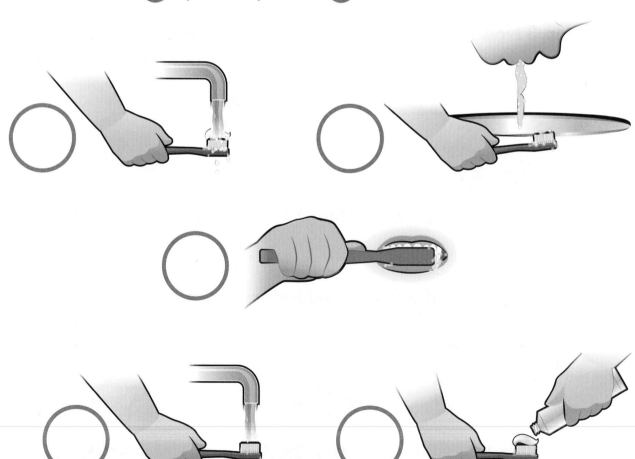

Tying Your Shoes

Tying Your Shoe: The **Bunny Ears** Method

Steps 1 & 2 First make a knot for the bunny's head.
Take the laces and cross them over to make an "X."
Then, pull one lace through the bottom of the "X" and pull tight.

Step 3 Now loop the laces into bunny ears.

Step 4 Make an "X" using the bunny ears.

Step 5 Slide one ear under the "X."

Step 6 Pull tightly.

Circle the picture that happened **before** Claire put on her shoes.

Family Members

Trace the names of family members below.

grandpa

mom

brother

dad

grandma

sister

My Family

How many people are in your family? _____

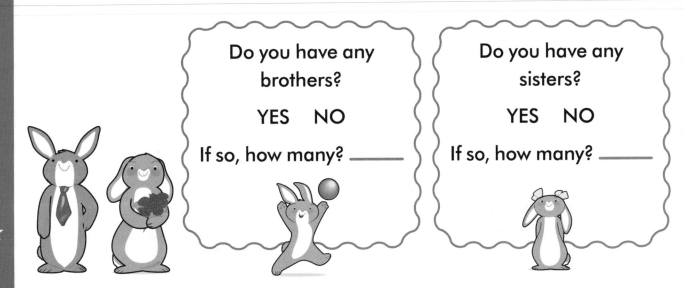

Do you have any brothers?

YES   NO

If so, how many? _____

Do you have any sisters?

YES   NO

If so, how many? _____

Draw your family in the house below.

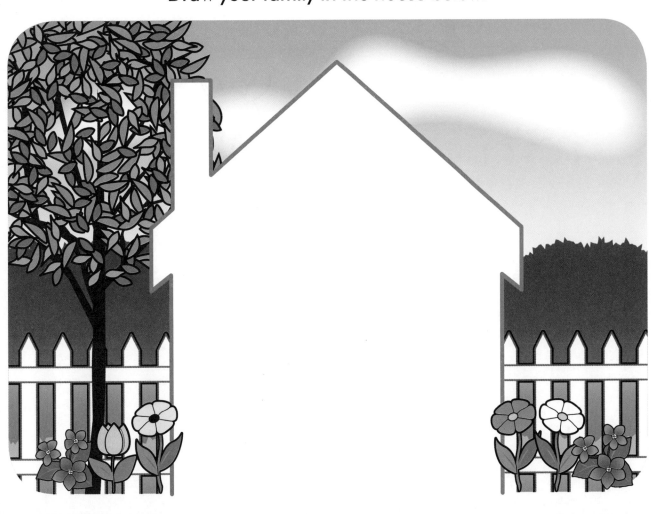

Car Safety

Whenever you ride in a car, you must sit in the back seat and wear your seat belt. Circle the picture below showing the right way to ride in a car.

Helmets

Helmets are important for safety.
Draw a line from the child with the **helmet** to
activities where a **helmet** must be worn.

**playing
basketball**

**riding a
scooter**

**riding in
a car**

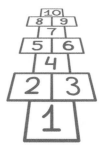

**riding a
skateboard**

**going to
the dentist**

**riding a
bike**

**playing
hopscotch**

Crossing the Street

Before you cross a street, Stop, Look, and Listen!

Draw a line from each word to its matching picture.

STOP

LOOK

LISTEN

When it comes to traffic lights, a red light means stop. A yellow light means slow down, and a green light means go.
Draw a line between the traffic light color and what it means.

GO **STOP** **SLOW**

Places in My Neighborhood

A **neighborhood** is an area of a town or city where people live. Besides many different types of homes, there are a lot of different businesses there too. Look at each place and then circle the object that goes with it.

People in My Neighborhood

There are many helpful people in your **neighborhood**. Match the helpers below with the object that goes with each one. Circle the correct answer.

What would you like to do when you grow up?

NATURE & SCIENCE

Animals and Their Babies

Are You My Mother?
Circle the correct baby to match its mother.

285

Animals and Their Babies

Are You My Mother?

Circle the correct baby to match its mother.

What Does the Fox Say?

Write what each animal says on the lines.

Moo

Baaa

Ribbit

Oink

Cock-a-doodle-doo

Quack

Woof

What does the
frog say?

_____

_____

What does the
duck say?

_____

_____

What does the
pig say?

_____

_____

What does the
dog say?

_____

_____

What does the
cow say?

_____

_____

What does the
sheep say?

_____

_____

What does the
rooster say?

_____

_____

Feathers, Fur, or Scales

All animals have special traits that make them different from one another, such as having feathers, fur, or scales.
Put the animals in the group where they belong.

Draw a square ■ around all animals with feathers.

Draw a circle ● around all animals with scales.

Draw a triangle ▲ around all animals with fur.

Animal Habitats: Forest

A **habitat** is where an animal lives. There are many different **habitats**. One **habitat** is a **forest**.

Forest animals

deer   owl   chipmunk   bear   squirrel

Color the fox in the **forest**.

Draw two animals that live in the **forest** and write their names.

I went to the forest and what did I see?

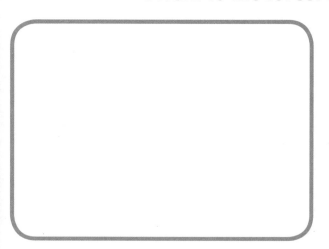

I saw a _____   I saw a _____
looking at me!   looking at me!

Animal Habitats: Savanna

A **savanna** is a hot, dry grassland found
in places like Madagascar.

Savanna animals

panther

zebra

jaguar

lion

giraffe

Color the
rhino in the
savanna.

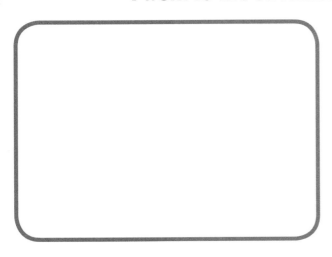
meerkat

Draw two animals that live in the **savanna** and write their names.

I went to the savanna and what did I see?

I saw a _____
looking at me!

I saw a _____
looking at me!

290

Animal Habitats: Ocean

Another **habitat** is the **ocean**.
Many animals live in the **ocean**.

Ocean animals

whale

sea turtle

crab

fish

seal

Color the shark in the **ocean**.

Draw two animals that live in the **ocean** and write their names.

I went to the ocean and what did I see?

I saw a _____
looking at me!

I saw a _____
looking at me!

Animal Habitats: Polar

Polar habitats are located at the very north and the very south of the globe. Both are very cold!

Polar animals

narwhal

walrus

polar fox

polar bear

Color the penguins in the **polar habitat**.

Draw two animals that live in **polar habitats** and write their names.

I went to the north pole and what did I see?

I went to the south pole and what did I see?

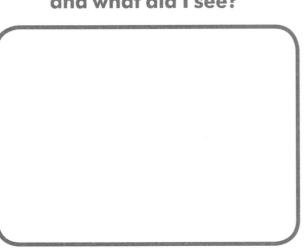

I saw a _____
looking at me!

I saw a _____
looking at me!

What Do Plants Need?

Plants need soil to grow. It provides nutrients, which is the plants' food.

Plants need sunlight for photosynthesis, which changes the nutrients in soil into energy to grow.

Water provides nutrients for the plants and helps break those nutrients down in the soil.

Label the pictures in order of 1 to 4 to show how a plant grows.

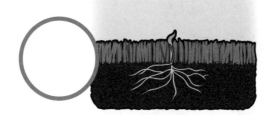

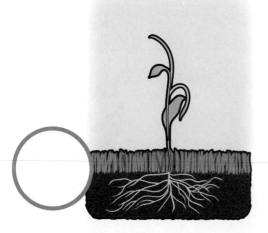

The Life Cycle of a Butterfly

Look at the butterfly life cycle stages.
Put the stage numbers in the circles below.

Stage 1 An egg is laid on a leaf, and a caterpillar is born from that egg.

Stage 2 The caterpillar spends most of its life eating leaves.

Stage 3 When it gets big enough, the caterpillar attaches itself to a twig and forms a chrysalis, or a cocoon.

Stage 4 Hatching out of the chrysalis is a beautiful butterfly!

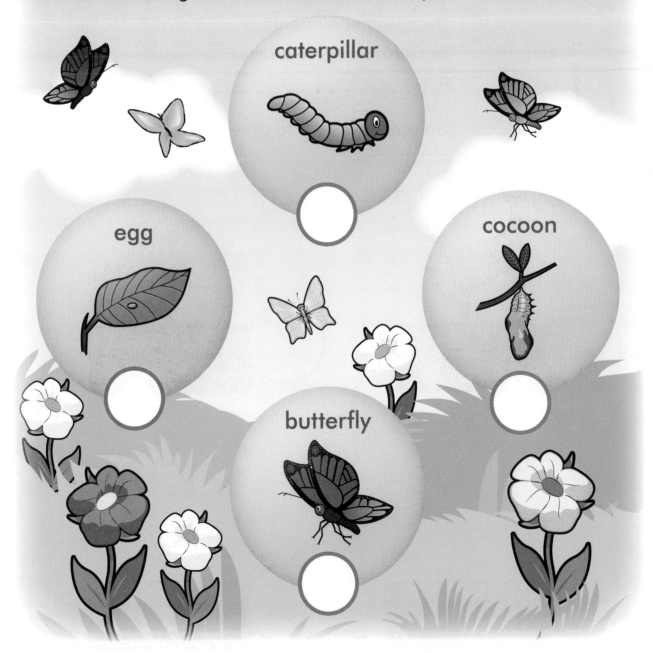

caterpillar

egg

cocoon

butterfly

The Four Seasons

Winter occurs in three months:
December   January   February
Below is a farm in **winter**.

Circle the words that describe the weather in **winter**.

Rainy   Hot

Windy   Cold

Snowy   Cool

Spring occurs in three months:
March   April   May
Below is a farm in **spring**.

Circle the words that describe the weather in **spring**.

Rainy   Hot

Windy   Cold

Snowy   Cool

The Four Seasons

Summer occurs in three months:

June   July   August

Below is a farm in **summer**.

Circle the words that describe the weather in **summer**.

Rainy   Hot

Windy   Cold

Snowy   Cool

Fall occurs in three months:

September   October   November

Below is a farm in **fall**.

Circle the words that describe the weather in **fall**.

Rainy   Hot

Windy   Cold

Snowy   Cool

The Four Seasons

Trace the season words. Then decorate each tree based on how you think it would look in that season.

Earth Day Every Day

Earth Day is on April 22 every year. **Earth Day** reminds us to take care of our planet by keeping it clean. Yet we should be doing that every day! We can do that by following a practice of **reduce**, **reuse**, and **recycle**.

 **Reduce**

 **Reuse**

 **Recycle**

Reduce means to use less of something, such as water.

Reuse means to use things again, instead of just throwing them away.

Recycle means to make something new from something old. We recycle bottles to make new bottles.

Look at the definitions above. Think of one example for each of how we can **reduce**, **reuse**, and **recycle**. Draw a picture of your examples in the boxes below.

Color in the 3 **R**'s sign below. What color? Green, of course!

Earth Day Every Day

Reduce, Reuse, Recycle
Sung to *Itsy Bitsy Spider*

Reduce, Reuse, Recycle—words that we all know.
We have to save our planet so we can live and grow.
We might be only small children, but we will try, you'll see.
And we can save this planet—it starts with you and me!

Help sort the garbage.
Draw a line from each item to either
the trash can or the recycling bin.

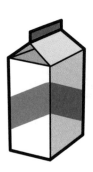

Solid, Liquid, and Gas

A **solid** is a form of matter that keeps its shape. A pencil is an example of a **solid**.

A **liquid** is a form of matter that takes the shape of its container. Orange juice is a **liquid** that takes the shape of its glass.

A **gas** is a form of matter that has no shape of its own. Steam from a hot drink is a **gas**.

Color all solids

Color all liquids

Color all gases

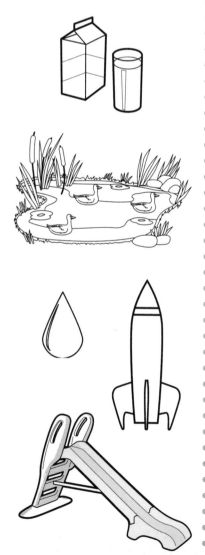

The Five Senses

Our Five Senses

We _____ with our .

We _____ with our .

We _____ with our .

We _____ with our 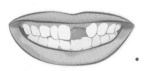 .

We _____ with our  .

The Five Senses

Draw a picture to go with each of the five senses.

I can hear...

I can see...

I can touch...

I can taste...

I can smell...

The Five Senses

On the spaces below, name one thing you can do with each of your five senses during a walk in the forest.

On a walk through the woods...

I could 👁 _____.

I could 👂 _____.

I could 👃 _____.

I could ✋ _____.

I could 👄 _____.

I think the most important sense
of the five senses is

_____

_____

because

_____

_____

ANSWER KEY

Page 11

Page 12

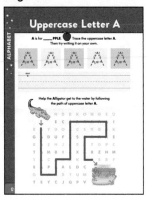

Page 13

Page 15

Page 16

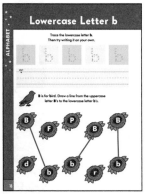

Page 17

Page 19

Page 20

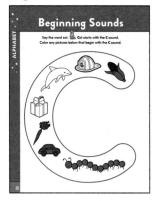

Page 21

Page 22

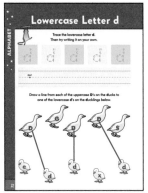

Page 23

Page 24

Page 25

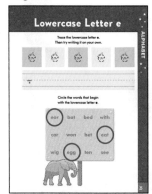

Page 26

Page 27

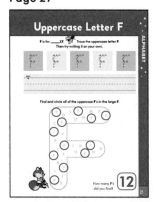

Page 28

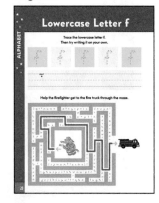

ANSWER KEY

Page 31

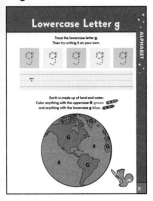

Page 32

Page 33

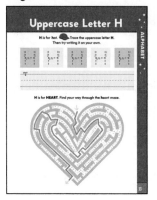

Page 34

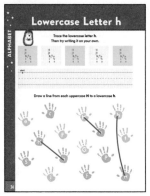

Page 35

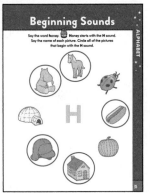

Page 36

Page 37

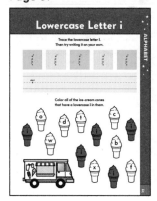

Page 38

Page 39

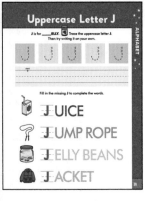

Page 40

Page 41

Page 42

Page 43

Page 44

Page 46

Page 47

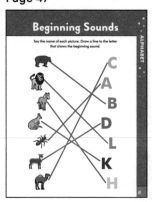

ANSWER KEY

Page 48

Page 49

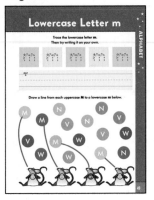

Page 51

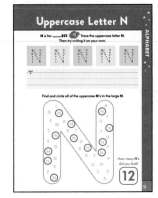

Page 52

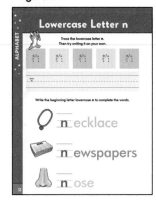

Page 53

Page 54

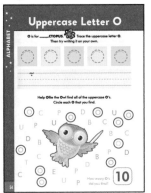

Page 55

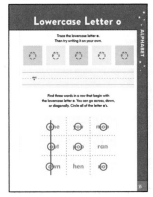

Page 56

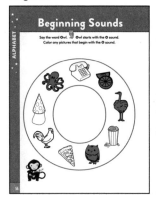

Page 58

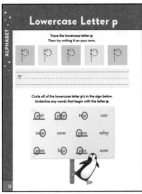

Page 59

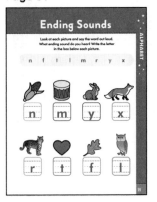

Page 60

Page 61

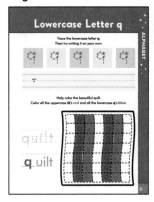

Page 62

Page 63

Page 64

Page 66

ANSWER KEY

Page 67

Lowercase Letter s

Page 68

Beginning Sounds

Page 69

Uppercase Letter T

Fill in the missing T to complete the words.

- TOP
- TIGER
- TREE
- TOMATO
- TRIANGLE

Page 70
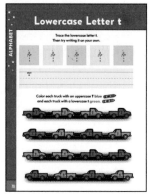
Lowercase Letter t

Page 71

Beginning Sounds

Page 72
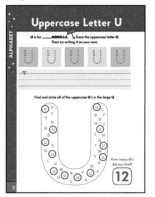
Uppercase Letter U

How many U's did you find? 12

Page 73

Lowercase Letter u

Page 74

Beginning Sounds

Qq
Rr
Ss
Tt
Uu

Page 75

Uppercase Letter V

How many V's did you find? 7

Page 76

Lowercase Letter v

Page 77

Beginning Sounds

Page 79

Lowercase Letter w

Page 80

Beginning Sounds

W S
W
S W
S

Page 81
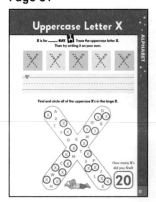
Uppercase Letter X

How many X's did you find? 20

Page 82

Lowercase Letter x

Page 83

Ending Sounds

x l f r k r

- fo x
- wol f
- dee r
- skun k
- squirre l
- bea r

ANSWER KEY

Page 84

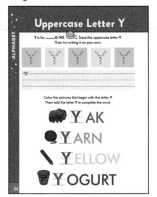

Page 85

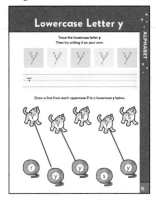

Page 86

Page 87

Page 91

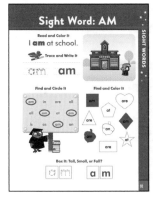

Page 92

Page 93

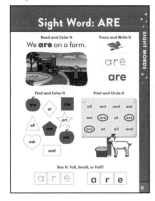

Page 94

Page 95

Page 97

Page 98

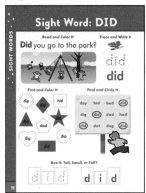

Page 99

Page 100

Page 101

Page 102

Page 103

ANSWER KEY

Page 104

Page 105

Page 106

Page 107

Page 109

Page 110

Page 111

Page 112

Page 113

Page 114

Page 115

Page 116

Page 117

Page 118
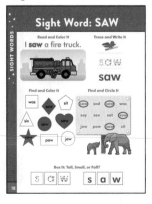

Page 119
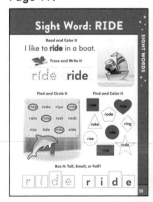

Page 120
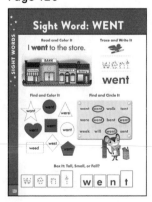

ANSWER KEY

Page 121

Page 122

Page 123

Page 124

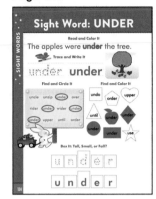

Page 125

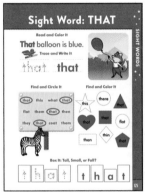

Page 126

Page 127

Page 128

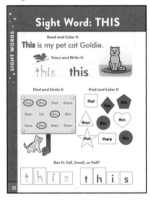

Page 129

Page 130

Page 131

Page 132

Page 133

Page 134

Page 135

Page 136

ANSWER KEY

Page 137

Page 138

Page 139

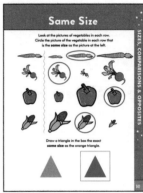

Page 141

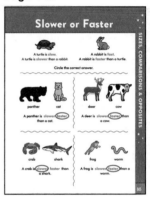

Page 142

Page 143

Page 144

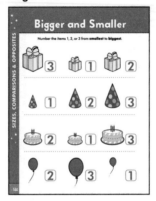

Page 145

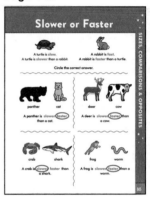

Page 146

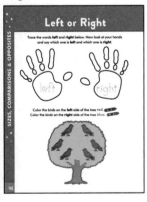

Page 147

Page 148

Page 149

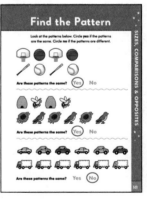

Page 150

Page 151

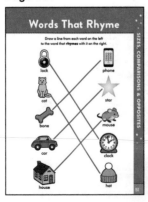

Page 152

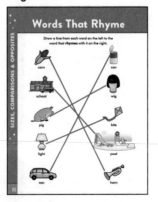

Page 153

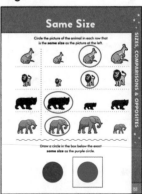

ANSWER KEY

Page 154

Page 155

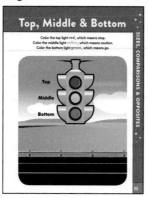

Page 156

Page 157

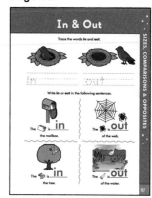

Page 158

Page 159

Page 160

Page 161

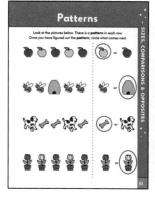

Page 162

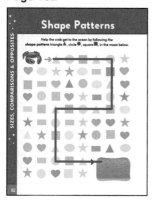

Page 163

Page 164

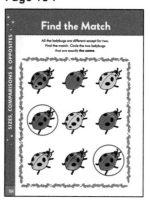

Page 165

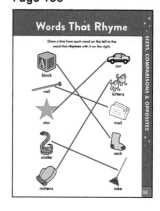

Page 166

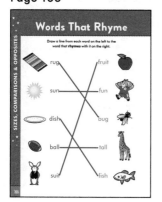

Page 167

Page 168

Page 169

ANSWER KEY

Page 170

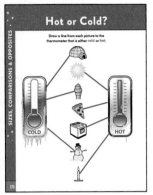

Page 171

Page 172

Page 173

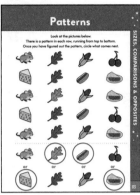

Page 174

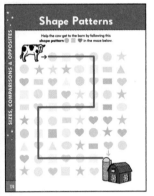

Page 175

Page 176

Page 178

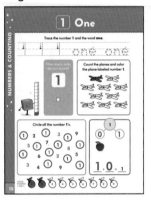

Page 179

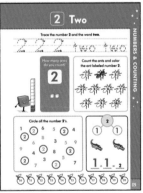

Page 180

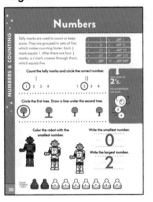

Page 181

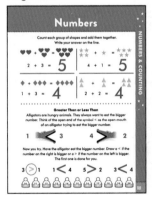

Page 182

Page 183

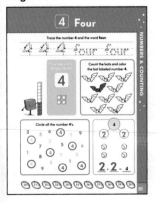

Page 184

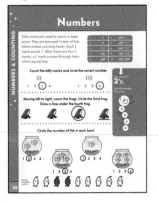

Page 185

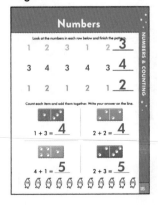

Page 186

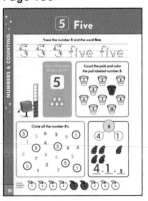

ANSWER KEY

Page 187

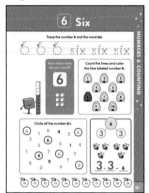

Page 188

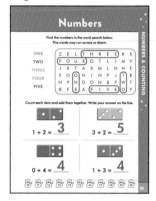

Page 189

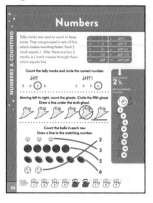

Page 190

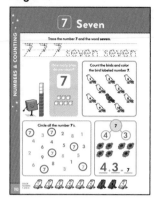

Page 191

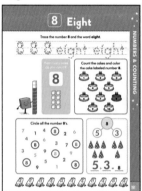

Page 192

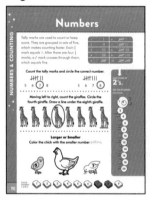

Page 193

Page 194

Page 195

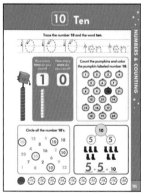

Page 196

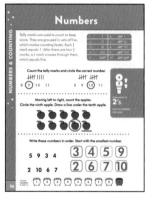

Page 197

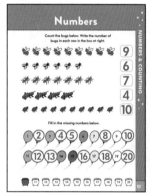

Page 198

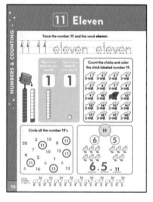

Page 199

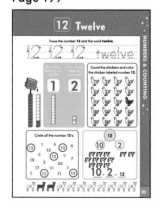

Page 200

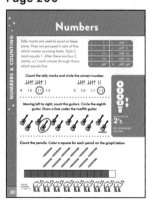

Page 201

Page 202

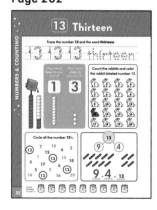

ANSWER KEY

Page 203

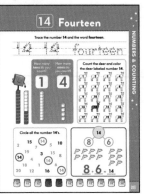

Page 204

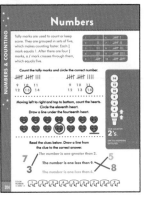

Page 205

Page 206

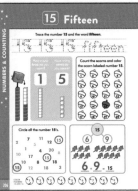

Page 207

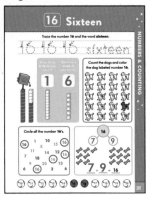

Page 208

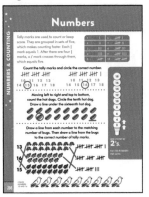

Page 209

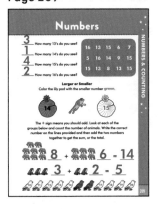

Page 210

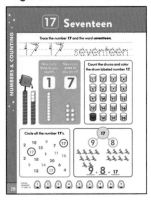

Page 211

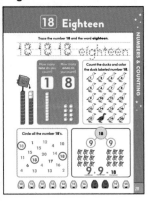

Page 212

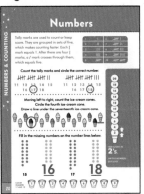

Page 213

Page 214

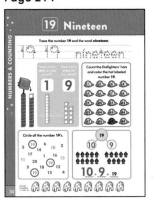

Page 215

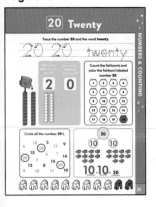

Page 216

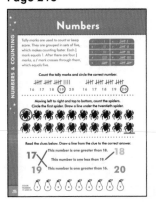

Page 217

Page 218

ANSWER KEY

Page 221

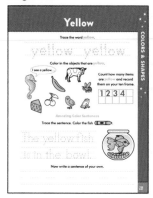

Page 222

Page 223

Page 224

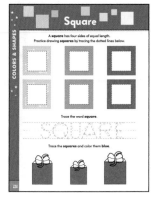

Page 225

Page 227

Page 228

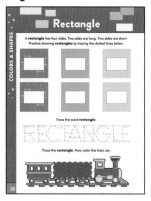

Page 229

Page 230

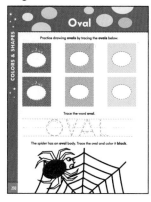

Page 231

Page 232

Page 233

Page 234

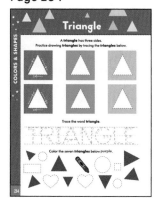

Page 235

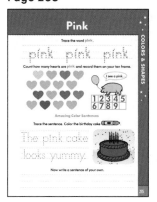

Page 236

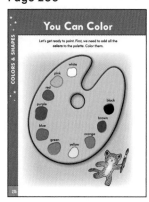

Page 237

ANSWER KEY

Page 238

Colors and Shapes

I Know My Colors and Shapes
Trace the shape words.

Square   Circle
Triangle   Heart

Color the squares green. How many are there? __12__
Color the triangles yellow. How many are there? __6__
Color the circles blue. How many are there? __5__
Color the hearts red. How many are there? __4__

Page 239

Colors and Shapes

I Know My Colors and Shapes
Trace the shape words.

Rectangle   Oval
Diamond   Heart

Color the rectangles purple. How many are there? __7__
Color the ovals orange. How many are there? __8__
Color the diamonds black. How many are there? __5__
Color the hearts pink. How many are there? __5__

Page 240

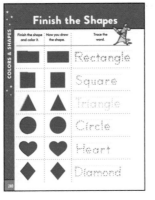

Finish the Shapes

Finish the shape and color it. Now you draw the shape. Trace the word.

Rectangle
Square
Triangle
Circle
Heart
Diamond

Page 241

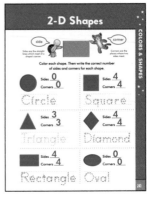

2-D Shapes

Sides are the straight lines which meet at a shape's corner.
Corners are the places where two sides meet.

Color each shape. Then write the correct number of sides and corners for each shape.

Circle — Sides 0, Corners 0
Square — Sides 4, Corners 4
Triangle — Sides 3, Corners 3
Diamond — Sides 4, Corners 4
Rectangle — Sides 4, Corners 4
Oval — Sides 0, Corners 0

Page 242

3-D Shapes

A sphere looks like a ball. Color the box that has an item shaped like a sphere.

Sphere

A cube looks like a wooden block. Color the box that has an item shaped like a cube.

Cube

A cylinder looks like a can of soda. Color the box that has an item shaped like a cylinder.

Cylinder

A cone looks like a bottom of an ice-cream cone. Color the box that has an item shaped like a cone.

Cone

Page 243

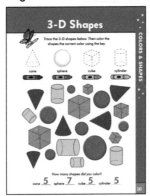

3-D Shapes

Trace the 3-D shapes below. Then color the shapes the correct color using the key.

cone   sphere   cube   cylinder

How many shapes did you color?
cone 5   sphere 7   cube 5   cylinder 5

Page 244

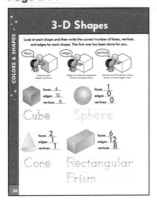

3-D Shapes

Look at each shape and then write the correct number of faces, vertices, and edges for each shape. The first one has been done for you.

Faces are the shape's surfaces.
Edges are the line segments where two faces meet.
Vertices are the places where three or more points meet.

Cube — faces 6, edges 12, vertices 8
Sphere — faces 0, edges 0, vertices 0
Cone — faces 2, edges 1, vertices 1
Rectangular Prism — faces 6, edges 12, vertices 8

Page 246

Telling Time

A clock shows twelve hours, which is half a day.
Fill in the missing hours.

Page 247

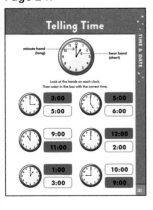

Telling Time

minute hand (long)   hour hand (short)

Look at the hands on each clock.
Then color in the box with the correct time.

3:00 / 5:00   5:00 / 6:00
9:00 / 12:00   11:00 / 2:00
1:00 / 10:00   3:00 / 9:00

Page 248

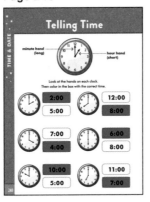

Telling Time

minute hand (long)   hour hand (short)

Look at the hands on each clock.
Then color in the box with the correct time.

2:00 / 12:00   5:00 / 8:00
7:00 / 6:00   4:00 / 8:00
10:00 / 11:00   5:00 / 7:00

Page 249

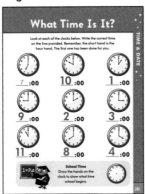

What Time Is It?

Look at each of the clocks below. Write the correct time on the line provided. Remember, the short hand is the hour hand. The first one has been done for you.

7:00   10:00   1:00
9:00   2:00   3:00
11:00   8:00   4:00

School Time
Draw the hands on the clock to show what time school begins.

Page 250

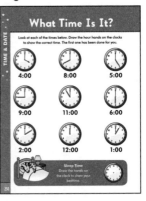

What Time Is It?

Look at each of the times below. Draw the hour hands on the clocks to show the correct time. The first one has been done for you.

4:00   8:00   5:00
9:00   11:00   6:00
2:00   1:00

Sleep Time
Draw the hands on the clock to show your bedtime.

Page 251

What Time Is It?

Look at the hands on each clock. Then draw a line to the box with its matching time. Remember, the small hand is the hour hand.

1:00 / 5:00
3:00 / 6:00
12:00 / 8:00

6:00 / 8:00
9:00 / 10:00
12:00 / 2:00

1:00 / 2:00
3:00 / 10:00
5:00 / 9:00

Page 252

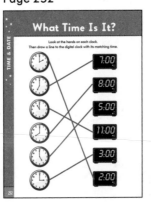

What Time Is It?

Look at the hands on each clock.
Then draw a line to the digital clock with its matching time.

7:00
8:00
5:00
11:00
3:00
2:00

Page 253

What Time Is It?

Look at each of the clocks below. Write the correct time on the line provided. Remember, the small hand is the hour hand. The first one has been done for you.

8:00   11:00   12:00
10:00   1:00   2:00
3:00   9:00   5:00

Lunchtime
Draw the hands on the clock to show what time you eat lunch.

Page 254

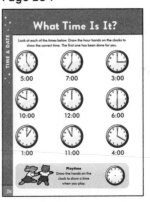

What Time Is It?

Look at each of the times below. Draw the hour hands on the clocks to show the correct time. The first one has been done for you.

5:00   7:00   3:00
10:00   12:00   6:00
1:00   11:00   4:00

Playtime
Draw the hands on the clock to show a time when you play.

ANSWER KEY

Page 256

Page 257

Page 258

Page 260

Page 261

Page 262

Page 265

Page 271
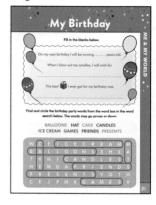

Page 272
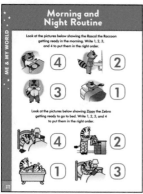

Page 273

Page 274
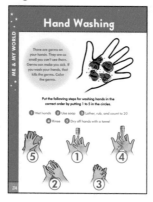

Page 275
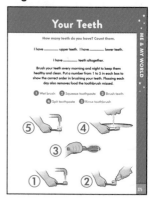

Page 276
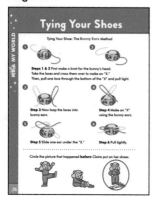

Page 279
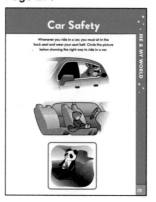

Page 280
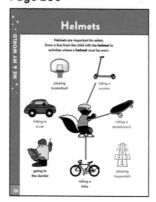

Page 281
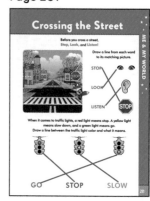

ANSWER KEY

Page 282

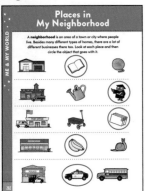
Places in My Neighborhood

Page 283

People in My Neighborhood

Page 285

Animals and Their Babies

Page 286

Animals and Their Babies

Page 287

What Does the Fox Say?

Page 288

Feathers, Fur, or Scales

Page 289

Animal Habitats: Forest

Page 293

What Do Plants Need?

Page 294

The Life Cycle of a Butterfly

Page 295

The Four Seasons

Page 296

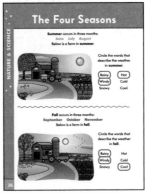
The Four Seasons

Page 297

The Four Seasons

Page 299

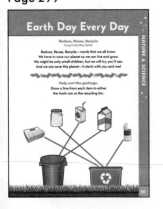
Earth Day Every Day

Page 300

Solid, Liquid, and Gas

Page 301

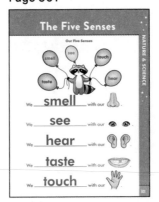
The Five Senses

Great Job!

_____

name

has completed all the exercises
in this workbook and is ready
for kindergarten.

_____

date

TEACHER APPROVED

GET READY FOR SCHOOL:
KINDERGARTEN

593 ACTIVITIES & 3,835 ILLUSTRATIONS